To Ken & ...

We ha... ...th

you in t... ...ek

and getting to know you. We have decided you are pretty special, and

You Are Special To God

A Scriptural Look at Why Man Is Special to God

Frank Richey 11-10-10

By
Frank Richey

Scripture Quotations

All of the scripture quotations are taken from the New King James
Version of the Bible, unless indicated otherwise.

For the help received in the printing of this book, I wish to thank
Bennie Johns of Baileyton, Alabama for the pre-press work.

ISBN 978-0-9816519-1-0

Published by
Cypress Creek Book Company
Florence, Alabama

Dedication

This book is dedicated to the memory of my sister, Nancy Richey, who came into this world with special challenges. As a child, she attended special classes. As an adult she painted special paintings and spread a special sunshine to others. Nancy was special to her family, special to her friends and special to her church family.

But most importantly, she **IS** "Special to God!"

"But you are a chosen generation, a royal priesthood, a holy nation, *His own special people*, that you may proclaim the praises of Him who called you out of darkness into His marvelous light."
1 Peter 2:9

"Who gave Himself for us, that He might redeem us from every lawless deed and purify for Himself *His own special people*, zealous for good works."
Titus 2:14

Table of Contents

Page

Introduction 7

You Are Special to God:

Because He Made You and Gave Your Life Purpose 17
Because He Wants To Dwell With You 27
Because He Wants You to Talk With Him 37
Because He Wants You to Hear Him............................... 49
Because He Provides For You 59
Because He Knows How You Feel................................... 69
Because His Son Died For You 81
Because His Church Was Built For You........................... 91
Because His Word Is Spread By You 99
Because His Son Is Your Shepherd 109
Because He Uses You to Influence Others for Good...... 123
Because He Has Shown You the Unseen 133

Epilogue...141

Introduction

You Are Special to God

"But you are a chosen generation, a royal priesthood, a holy nation, His own special people, that you may proclaim the praises of Him who called you out of darkness into His marvelous light."

1 Peter 2:9

It sounds strange doesn't it? Say it to yourself—"I am special to God!" Perhaps it is hard to say. To do so, conjures up the idea of one's own personal self-esteem, arrogance, haughtiness, superiority, and pride. In light of so many Bible passages that teach that Christians are to be humble, lowly and meek, how can one have the audacity to proclaim that he is special? Can one say, "I am special to God" and mean it and still fulfill the biblical admonitions of humility? I believe so.

Because of the nature of the material presented in this book, I believe it necessary to preface the material with an apology. Not an apology in the sense of expressing regret or asking pardon for a fault or offense, but an apology in the sense of a formal defense or justification of a position (appologia-gk., apo-defense + logos-discourse, speech).

7

This material is dedicated to the "other side of the coin." Most of us have been taught the biblical principles of humility and of esteeming others better than ourselves (Romans 12:3; Philippians 2:3), but we have not focused on other passages of scripture that teach that we, the highest form of creation, are special to God. In fact, there are many Bible passages that make this point.

In the Old Testament, we have several passages that point out how God's people are special to Him. Several times His people are referred to as a **"special treasure."** God said that those who obey His voice and keep His covenant **"shall be a special treasure to Me** above all people..." (Exodus 19:5). In Deuteronomy 7:6, Moses said, "...your God has chosen you to be a people for Himself, **a special treasure** above all the peoples on the face of the earth." Deuteronomy 14:2 tells us that "...you are a holy people to the Lord your God, and the Lord has chosen you to be a people for Himself, **a special treasure** above all the peoples who are on the face of the earth." Psalm 135:4 says, "For the Lord has chosen Jacob for Himself, Israel for **His special treasure.**"

The New Testament also points out that we are special to God. We have the word of our Lord Jesus Christ and of His chosen apostles, Peter and John. Jesus, in the Sermon on the Mount, pointed out that we are **"the salt of the earth"** (Matthew 5:13) and **"the light of the world"** (Matthew 5:14). Certainly this focuses on the fact that God's people have a special purpose on earth—a purpose to influence the world for good.

The expression, "special to God," is found twice in the Bible in the New King James Version. First, let us consider 1 Peter 2:9 which says, "But you are a chosen generation, a royal priesthood, a holy nation, **His own special people**, that you may proclaim the praises of Him who called you out of darkness into His marvelous light." The American Standard Version translates this as "a people for [God's] own possession" while the Revised Standard Version says, "a people for possession." The King James Version says, "a peculiar people." Albert Barnes commenting on this part of the passage said, "The word peculiar, in its common acceptation now, would mean that they were distinguished from others, or were singular. The reading in the margin would mean that they had been bought or redeemed. Both these things are so, but neither of them expresses the exact sense of the original. The meaning is, 'a people for a possession;' that is, as pertaining to God. They are a people which He has secured as a possession, or as His own; a people, therefore, which belong to Him, and to no other. In this sense they are peculiar as being His; and, being such, it may be inferred that they should be peculiar in the sense of being unlike others in their manner of life. But that idea is not necessarily in the text. There seems to be here also an allusion to Exodus 19:5: **'Ye shall be a peculiar treasure with me above all people'**" (Albert Barnes Commentary).

We do not need to leave this passage without mentioning the other phrases that point out how special we are to God. Peter also points out that we are a **"chosen generation,"** a **"royal priesthood,"** and a **"holy nation."** Without going into detail, these designations certainly speak to the fact that we are special to God.

Next, consider Titus 2:14, which says, "who gave Himself for us, that He might redeem us from every lawless deed and purify for Himself **His own special people**, zealous for good works." The People's New Testament Commentary says concerning His own special people, that God's people are a "peculiar people; separate, chosen, holy in life. The Jews were, under the old covenant, a peculiar people; now, Christians are God's Israel." According to this passage, these "special people" are zealous for good works. Good works is a recurring theme in the book of Titus, and certainly those that are special to God will busy themselves doing good works.

To say "I am special to God" does not take away from the glory and majesty of Jehovah, the God of the Universe—the El Shaddai, the Almighty God! To recognize oneself as special is, in actuality, a tribute to our God on high.

The scriptures are legion that show the special relationship God has with His people. Some examples are that God sanctifies us (John 17:19); we, as members of His church, were purchased with His own blood (Acts 20:28); He has reserved an inheritance for us in heaven (1 Peter 1:3-4); we are God's temple (1 Corinthians 3:17); He has "delivered us from the power of darkness and conveyed us into the kingdom of the Son of His love" (Colossians 1:13); He has made us "kings and priests" (Revelation 1:6; 5:10).

We are also told that we will "judge the world" and "judge the angels" (1 Corinthians 6:2-3); that we are "heirs of God through Christ" (Galatians 4:7), and that we are "children of God" and "joint heirs with Christ" (Romans 8:16-17). We also see from Ephesians 3:20 that we have abundant power. "Now to Him who is able to do exceedingly abundantly above all that we ask or think, according to the power that works in us."

These passages teach that we are kings, priests, sons of God, heirs of God, adopted of God, children of God, a chosen generation, a royal priesthood, a holy nation, a special people. They also teach that we are powerful and that we will judge the world and the angels.

The focus of this material is not to diminish for one instant the importance of God in our lives but to emphasize that we are **SPECIAL TO GOD**! For too long we have sold ourselves short on the power, abilities, and possibilities that God has given us. Isn't it about time we realized the power we have as children of God? Isn't it time to realize that we are important and that we are special and that God has by design and decree made us and our relationship "Special to God"?

But, Without God I Am Not Very Special

As we are discussing the subject of being special to God, let us never forget that without God we are not worth much. Without God we are vile, wretched creatures with no hope. Man's faith alone will not save him. Indeed, James said "faith without works is dead" (James 2:17, 20, 26). Man's works alone will not save him. The grace of our God extended to mankind, demonstrated by the sending of His son to die for us, and has brought us near to Him by the blood of Christ (Ephesians 2:13).

Read Matthew 19:16-26. In this passage, a rich man came to Jesus inquiring as to what he must do in order to have eternal life. This was a noble question, but the man was not pleased when the Lord told him to "go, sell what you have and give to the poor" (v.21). Even the disciples of Jesus were amazed at the answer that Jesus gave. Notice verse 26, where Jesus says, "With men this is impossible; but with God all things are possible."

Let us look at some examples of biblical characters who were great men of faith, but they were not special without God.

Without God, Noah Was Not Special

God had determined to destroy man but Noah found grace in the sight of God. The Bible tells us, "Then the LORD saw that the wickedness of man was great in the earth, and that every intent of the thoughts of his heart was only evil continually. And the LORD was sorry that He had made man on the earth, and He was grieved in His heart. So the LORD said, 'I will destroy man whom I have created from the face of the earth, both man and beast, creeping thing and birds of the air, for I am sorry that I have made them.' But Noah found grace in the eyes of the LORD" (Genesis 6:5-8).

God gave Noah instructions and Noah followed them. The Hebrews writer tells us, "By faith Noah, being divinely warned of things not yet seen, moved with godly fear, prepared an ark for the saving of his household, by which he condemned the world and became heir of the righteousness which is according to faith" (Hebrews 11:7).

Noah's faith was in God, not in himself. With God, nothing is impossible. Without God, I am nothing.

Without God, Abraham Was Not Special

God called Abraham when he was in the city of Ur. Abraham was a nomadic shepherd. He had amassed wealth, but without God, he was not special. Notice how God changed Abraham's life. "Now the LORD had said to Abram: 'Get out of your country, from your family and from your father's house, To a land that I will show you. I will make you a great nation; I will bless you and make your name great; and you shall be a blessing. I will bless those who bless you, and I will curse him who curses you; and in you all the families of the earth shall be blessed.' So Abram departed as the LORD had spoken to him, and Lot went with him. And Abram was seventy-five years old when he departed from Haran" (Genesis 12:1-4).

Abraham was a man of great faith. He learned that he must depend on God. You don't find Abraham talking about what he had accomplished in life. He allowed God to direct his life.

Abraham was searching for something more than a home on this earth. He was searching for an eternal home—a home in heaven that would be everlasting. We are told that "By faith he dwelt in the land of promise as in a foreign country, dwelling in tents with Isaac and Jacob, the heirs with him of the same promise; for he waited for the city which has foundations, whose builder and maker is God" (Hebrews 11:9-10).

Abraham has often been referred to as the "father of the faithful." This man had such great faith. Even when God tested him by the offering of his son as a sacrifice, Abraham did not hesitate to carry out God's orders. We are told, "when he was tested, offered up Isaac, and he who had received the promises offered up his only begotten son," and that Abraham had concluded before hand "that God was able to raise him up, even from the dead, from which he also received him in a figurative sense." (Hebrews 11:17-19). Like Abraham, we are to be men and women of faith, always willing to do the will of God in all things, even when it is unpopular with the majority.

Without God, Daniel Was Not Special

Daniel was one of the great men of faith in the Old Testament. When the corrupt politicians of the day arranged for Daniel's demise, God saved His servant. Take time to read Daniel, Chapter 6. Notice the impact that Daniel had already made on King Darius, when the king said to Daniel, "Your God, whom you serve continually, He will deliver you" (Daniel 6:16). After Daniel survived the ordeal of spending the night in the lion's den, Darius said, "I make a decree that in every dominion of my kingdom men must tremble and fear before the God of Daniel. For He is the living God, and steadfast forever; His kingdom is the one which shall not be destroyed, and His dominion shall endure to the end. He delivers and rescues, and He works signs and wonders in heaven and on earth, Who has delivered Daniel from the power of the lions" (Daniel 6:26-27).

Notice that in these passages, the credit for the deliverance of Daniel was given to God by King Darius. Both Daniel and Darius knew that Daniel was delivered from the lions' den by the power of God. Without God, Daniel would have been destroyed.

Daniel was a great man who loved and served God, but without God, Daniel was not special. We also must realize that whatever great things we accomplish in life, we are nothing without God.

Without God, Peter Was Not Special

Peter was one of the great leaders in the New Testament church. He was the principal speaker when the church was established in Acts 2. When Peter was arrested following the death of James, he knew he was facing the same fate. When he was miraculously delivered, he knew that this was the work of God. This story is recorded for us in Acts 12: 1-19. Notice in particular, verse 11. "And when Peter had come to himself, he said, 'Now I know for certain that the Lord has sent His angel, and has delivered me from the hand of Herod and *from* all the expectation of the Jewish people'" (Acts 12:11).

Peter knew that his deliverance was from God, and gave credit to God for his deliverance. Peter, without God, was not special.

Conclusion

Yes, the Bible teaches that we are "special to God." But the thing we must understand is that we are "special to God" because of our relationship with God. Without that relationship, we are not special. We must accept God at His word. Accept the fact that when we have a relationship with God, we are His own special people.

In the material that is to follow, we are going to look at some of the ways in which we are special to God. But if you ever question whether you are special to God, focus on the fact that God thought we were worth saving, even when we were sinners and undeserving of salvation. The apostle Paul tells us, "For when we were still without strength, in due time Christ died for the ungodly. For scarcely for a righteous man will one die; yet perhaps for a good man someone would even dare to die. But God demonstrates His own love toward us, in that while we were still sinners, Christ died for us. Much more then, having now been justified by His blood, we shall be saved from wrath through Him" (Romans 5:6-9). Paul also tells us that, "In Him we have redemption through His blood, the forgiveness of sins, according to the riches of His grace" (Ephesians 1:7).

How thankful we should be that our Lord left the joys of heaven, came to this earth, and gave Himself as a sacrifice for us. We don't deserve this great blessing, and we should never ignore the love and concern that God has for His creation. We show our appreciation to Him by our complete and devoted service in His cause. I am thankful that God made us in such a way that we can be "Special to God."

Chapter 1

You Are Special to God Because He Made You and Gave Your Life Purpose

"In the beginning God created the heavens and the earth."

Genesis 1:1

We can so easily understand why couples desire to have children. For most married couples, this desire is to fulfill emptiness in their lives. Children can fill a void in their lives, bring joy to parents, and give life greater meaning. Is it so hard then to understand that God wanted children—a people He could call His own?

God created you. He brought you into existence. And because of that, "**You are Special to God.**" The creation must have been a special moment for God, as He set in order His plan for mankind.

The book of Genesis gives the account of the creation. Verse one tells us He "created the heavens and the earth. " Verses 26-28 say, "Then God said, 'Let Us make man in Our image, according to Our likeness; let them have dominion over the fish of the sea, over the birds of the air, and over the cattle, over all the earth and over every creeping thing that creeps on the earth.' So God created man in His own image; in the image of God He created him; male and female He created them. Then God blessed them, and God said to them, 'Be fruitful and multiply; fill the earth and subdue it; have dominion over the fish of the sea, over the birds of the air, and over every living thing that moves on the earth.'"

Chapter two of the Book of Genesis is significant in that it tells us that man was different from all other animal life. "And the LORD God formed man of the dust of the ground, and breathed into his nostrils the breath of life; and man became a living being" (Genesis 2:7). We are not the result of some cataclysmic freak of nature; we did not come from a one-celled organism in a dark slimy pond. We were created by Jehovah God! To deny such is to deny the Bible as the infallible, inerrant, all-sufficient word of God, directed by the Holy Spirit and given to man.

A Monkey Tale
By Frank Richey

An explosion in the universe
Took place so long ago,
So the evolutionists converse
And vow it must be so.

A fiery mass from the sun
Through heaven's sky did race.
It stopped and cooled. Life was begun.
The amoeba found its place.

It swam through oceans of the earth,
Dividing, growing as it went.
Procreating and giving birth
Until a billion years were spent.

Then crawled from water onto land
And shed fin and gill and scale,
Developed lungs in the beach's sun
And hair and ropey tail.

A billion years came to pass
Before the monkey in the tree,
Stood erect, they say, alas,
And walked like you and me.

Then down the tree the monkey came
And shed hair and ropey tail,
And man and monkey were not the same,
But the change was to no avail.

For man is still a monkey
If he believes this monkey tale,
And his life is lived in folly
And his soul is doomed to hell.

For God created all...,
And all includes the man.
And if in this simple truth we fall,
We miss the Master's plan.

God Is Our Creator

God is our creator. We weren't brought about as a result
of an explosion in the universe or as a result of billions of
years of evolution. "So God created man in His own image;
in the image of God He created him; male and female He
created them" (Genesis 1:27). After God created man, the

Bible tells us that "…God saw everything that He had made, and indeed it was very good…" (Genesis 1:31). To deny the creation of God is to deny the power—the omnipotence of God. Evolutionism says "God didn't bring all these things into existence." Some counter with theistic evolution in which they teach God used evolution to bring about His creation. Again, this limits God's power to speak things into existence.

By the power of the Almighty God of heaven, all of creation was spoken into existence. Notice some of the scriptural evidence of the creation given in the Book of Psalms:

Psalm 89:47 Remember how short my time is; for what futility have You created all the children of men?

Psalm 100:3 Know that the LORD, He is God; It is He who has made us, and not we ourselves; we are His people and the sheep of His pasture.

Psalm 104:30 You send forth Your Spirit, they are created; and You renew the face of the earth.

Psalm 148:5 Let them praise the name of the LORD, For He commanded and they were created.

The Bible tells us God knew us after we were conceived and before we were born. If anyone doubts that life begins at conception, spend some time with Psalm 139. The psalmist tells us that "You formed my inward parts; You covered me in my mother's womb." We are told that before birth "My frame was not hidden from You," and "Your eyes saw my substance, being yet unformed" (Psalm 139:13-16).

This psalm teaches that God knew us before our parents knew us. He formed us. He is the one that gave life. I am and you are special indeed, because God made us!

Why Did God Make You?

In all the years I have been in Bible classes where the discussion of creation came up, the most commonly asked questions are: <u>WHEN</u> did the creation take place and <u>WHERE</u> did the creation take place? It is strange to me that I have never heard anyone ask <u>WHY</u> the creation took place. I suggest that in order to understand why we are special to God we need to explore why God made us. On one occasion, I was told that if God didn't tell us, it is none of our business. This seemed to be a reference to Deuteronomy 29:29 which says "the secret things belong to God." However, the rest of that verse says, "the things that are revealed belong to us and to our children forever, that we may do all the words of this law."

Yes, there are secret things that belong to God, and there are "those things which are revealed" that "belong unto us and to our children forever." Therefore, from those things revealed concerning the creation of man, we can understand why God created man. The reason God made man is simply because He wanted to. God wanted to create man for His pleasure. John writes, "Thou art worthy, O Lord, to receive glory and honour and power: for thou hast created all things, and for thy pleasure they are and were created (Revelation 4:11-KJV).

Not only did God create man, but He gave man a purpose for living. Do you know why you are on this earth? Have you given thought to "What is your purpose in life?" Let's continue to explore the scriptures for the answers to these, and to similar questions.

Sometimes
By Frank Richey

Sometimes I just think it is a crime
That folks look back to the beginning of time;
And think they came from a dark pond's slime,
Instead of the God of Heaven, sublime.

Sometimes the story of the monkey in the tree,
Jumping down to the ground and becoming me,
Is pretty far fetched, as far as I can see.
It leaves God out of the picture, from A to Z.

Sometimes I just think that folks would be
Inclined to understand their sins and see,
That science offers not salvation free.
It is found in God, not the monkey.

Sometimes I think that folks could trust
That man was fashioned from lowly dust,
And not by chance as the evolutionists must,
But by the One who is Righteous, Holy and Just.

Sometimes look up on a starlit night,
And fathom the beauty, and glory, and might,
And notice the design and order are just right,
Made by the One Whose word made the light.

The Purpose of Man's Existence

Since God made man, certainly he gave man a purpose for living. Seemingly, man has lost his purpose in life. People are confronted with the questions, "What am I doing here?" and "What is my purpose in life?" This is evident in the number of suicides. People choose not to live because their life has no purpose. Over 1,000,000 people in the world kill themselves every year. In America, over 30,000 take their own lives. The number is probably far greater. Many take their own lives in ways that are often attributed to accidents instead of suicide. This great number of suicides should convince us that people have forgotten why they are on this globe. Without purpose in life and without a view of eternity, there is not much to live for on this earth.

Solomon, King of Israel, was the wisest of all men (1 Kings 4:29). In the Book of Ecclesiastes, Solomon explores the purpose of man's existence. In chapter one, Solomon uses three examples to show that in life, we "just go around and around." In verse five, he says, "The sun also rises, and the sun goes down, and hastens to the place where it arose," just like in the song in Fiddler on the Roof, "Sunrise, Sunset, Sunrise, Sunset." In verse 6, he says, "The wind goes toward the south, and turns around to the north; the wind whirls about continually, and comes again on its circuit." Again, we are like the wind, just going around and around. In verse 7, he uses this illustration: "All the rivers run into the sea, yet the sea *is* not full; to the place from which the rivers come, there they return again." Three times Solomon's illustrations point to the same thing—in life we are just going around in circles. Do you feel like that sometimes—that you are just going around in circles with no purpose in life? You get up in the morning, dress, eat, rush to work or school, come home, eat, watch TV, and go to bed. The next day you do the same thing—and the next—and soon you look back on life and say, "Is that all there is?"

Once Solomon concluded that his life is just going around in circles, he decided to do something about it. He decides the purpose of life must be in material possessions, wine, women and song. In chapter two of Ecclesiastes, that is what he pursues. He says in verse 3, "I searched in my heart *how* to gratify my flesh with wine, while guiding my heart with

23

wisdom, and how to lay hold on folly, till I might see what *was* good for the sons of men to do under heaven all the days of their lives" (Ecclesiastes 2:3). Solomon's philosophy was come on baby, let the good times roll. Eat, drink, and party hardy, because tomorrow this could all be over with. Does that sound like people today?

Solomon built houses and planted vineyards (v. 4), made gardens and orchards (v. 5), pools of water (v. 6), had a number of servants and great possessions. His cattle were more than had ever been in Jerusalem before him (v. 7). He gathered silver, gold, and peculiar treasures of kings; had singers and all sorts of instrumental accompaniments (v. 8). He was the richest man in Jerusalem (v. 9). Whatever his eyes desired, he did not keep it from them (v.10). And when all was said and done, his life was a useless bore. In verse 11, he said, "Then I looked on all the works that my hands had done and on the labor in which I had toiled; and indeed all *was* vanity and grasping for the wind. *There was* no profit under the sun." Solomon basically said there is no purpose in life. But as he continues searching for and exploring the purpose of life, he arrives at a conclusion in chapter 12. And his conclusion is one that should cause each of us to examine the things learned by Solomon.

Was Solomon so different from us? Man is constantly looking for purpose in life in having a good time, accumulating "toys," building up CD's and stock portfolios. He is seeking pleasure in alcohol and sexual fornication. He seeks pleasure in the trips he takes, and in the things he possesses. I read a statement on the front of a T-shirt one time that said, "He who collects the most toys wins." On the back it said, "But when the one who collects the most toys dies, he is still dead." If this constitutes our purpose in life, then our lives are indeed shallow and not of much value.

When Solomon comes to the end of the Book of Ecclesiastes, he has figured out the purpose of life. In

Ecclesiastes 11:9, he says, "Rejoice, O young man, in your youth, and let your heart cheer you in the days of your youth; walk in the ways of your heart, and in the sight of your eyes; But know that for all these God will bring you into judgment." Now Solomon has life figured out. Judgment must be a part of the picture and judgment changes everything. In chapter 12, he admonishes the young to "remember now your Creator in the days of your youth" (v. 1), and concludes his search of life's purpose with this statement: "Let us hear the conclusion of the whole matter: Fear God and keep His commandments, for this is man's all. For God will bring every work into judgment, including every secret thing, whether good or evil" (Ecclesiastes 12:13-14).

If we live our lives in view of a judgment, that changes everything—what we think, read, see, and hear, where we go and what we do. To ACCEPT judgment as a reality is to realize that man's purpose in life is to live life in such a way as to please God. In view of judgment, every action has eternal consequences.

The Judgment

Let us not kid ourselves about the subject of The Judgment. It is as real as anything you will experience in this life. Judgment is mentioned 312 times in the Bible and is therefore an important biblical topic. The "Day of Judgment" is mentioned eleven times in the New Testament. The final judgment of God is not a subject that people want to think about, but the Bible says we will all be there and give an account of the lives we have lived. "For we must all appear before the judgment seat of Christ, that each one may receive the things *done* in the body, according to what he has done, whether good or bad" (2 Corinthians 5:10).

John was allowed in a vision to see the judgment scene. He said, "Then I saw a great white throne and Him who sat on it, from whose face the earth and the heaven fled away. And there was found no place for them. And I saw the dead, small and great, standing before God, and books were opened. And another book was opened, which is *the Book* of Life. And the dead were judged according to their works, by the things which were written in the books. The sea gave up the dead who were in it, and Death and Hades delivered up the dead who were in them. And they were judged, each one according to his works. Then Death and Hades were cast into the lake of fire. This is the second death. And anyone not found written in the Book of Life was cast into the lake of fire" (Revelation 20:11-15).

Notice that we will be judged "by the things written in the books." What are these books? These are the books of the Bible. This should cause us to desire to read and study God's Word (His books) daily and in great detail, in order to know God's will and live it out in our lives each day.

Notice also that hell is described as a "lake of fire." This description certainly is one of great pain and anguish and a place we must avoid at all costs. If we lose our souls, we have lost it all.

Conclusion

Yes, God created us. He gave us purpose in life. He loved us and gave His Son, Jesus Christ, as atonement for our sins. It is beyond comprehension that God's only Son would die for His creation, yet that is how much God loved us and still loves us. Surely we are "Special to God."

Chapter 2

You Are Special to God Because He Wants to Dwell with You

"I will set My tabernacle among you, and My soul shall not abhor you. I will walk among you and be your God, and you shall be My people."

Leviticus 26:11-12

Have you ever thought that God, since the creation of man, desired to dwell with man and have man dwell with Him? The Bible is filled with stories of God's attempts to dwell with man and man's rejection of God. How it must have hurt God when man rejected Him and refused to allow God to dwell with him.

Evidence of God's desire to dwell with man is seen in the very beginning of time in the Garden of Eden. The relationship between man and God was special. In a sense, God dwelt with Adam and Eve in the garden. It seemed to be customary for God to converse with them. Notice that

27

after Adam and Eve had sinned, they hid themselves from God. Why? Perhaps because it was such a common thing for God to come into the Garden of Eden and dwell with them, speaking to them on a regular basis. "And they heard the sound of the LORD God walking in the garden in the cool of the day, and Adam and his wife hid themselves from the presence of the LORD God among the trees of the garden. Then the LORD God called to Adam and said to him, 'Where are you?'" (Genesis 3:8-9). I do not believe that God did not know where they were. He was simply starting a conversation with them. Prior to sin in the garden, a beautiful relationship existed between man and God as God dwelt with Adam and Eve.

But sin severed this relationship. It is man's sin that separates him from God: "But your iniquities have separated you from your God; and your sins have hidden His face from you, so that He will not hear" (Isaiah 59:2).

As the Genesis account continues in Genesis, chapter 3, we have the story of the sin of Adam and Eve and the falling away; in chapter 4, Cain kills Abel; chapter 6 tells us that by that time the world was so evil that God decided to destroy it and save Noah and his family; chapter 9 mentions the sin of Noah and the curse of Ham and chapter 11 tells of the Tower of Babel and the attempt of people to reach heaven before God confounded their speech. In chapter 12, God puts into motion a plan to dwell with man.

God Calls Abraham

"Now the LORD had said to Abram: 'Get out of your country, from your family and from your father's house, to a land that I will show you. I will make you a great nation; I will bless you and make your name great; and you shall be a blessing. I will bless those who bless you, and I will curse him who curses you; and in you all the families of the earth shall be blessed'" (Genesis 12:1-3). Notice that there are three distinct promises in this passage. There is the land promise, the nation promise, and the promise that through Abraham, all nations of the earth would be blessed. All three of these promises have been fulfilled. God gave the land of Canaan to the descendants of Abraham. He gave Abraham a son from which a great nation came forth; and one of his descendants was Jesus Christ, who blesses all nations of the earth.

God Plans to Dwell With Abraham's Descendants

After God led His people out of Egyptian bondage, God, through His grace, took a great step to rectify what had happened in Genesis 3. The Children of Israel had become a great nation just as God promised and once again God demonstrated His desire to dwell with His people. This was to be accomplished through the building of The Tabernacle, a portable building that the Children of Israel could carry with them as they wandered in the Wilderness of Sinai. God promised to dwell with his people in the tabernacle. God said, "And let them make Me a sanctuary, that I may dwell among them. According to all that I show you, that is, the pattern of the tabernacle and the pattern of all its furnishings, just so you shall make it" (Exodus 25:8-9). In Leviticus 26:11-12, God said, "I will set My tabernacle among you, and My soul shall not abhor you. I will walk among you and be your God, and you shall be My people."

God Dwelling With His People Was Conditional

God promised to dwell among His people as long as they were faithful to Him. If the people became unfaithful, God said He would leave. Notice Leviticus 26:27-33: "And after all this, if you do not obey Me, but walk contrary to Me, then I also will walk contrary to you in fury; and I, even I, will chastise you seven times for your sins. You shall eat the flesh of your sons, and you shall eat the flesh of your daughters. I will destroy your high places, cut down your incense altars, and cast your carcasses on the lifeless forms of your idols; and My soul shall abhor you. I will lay your cities waste and bring your sanctuaries to desolation, and I will not smell the fragrance of your sweet aromas. I will bring the land to desolation, and your enemies who dwell in it shall be astonished at it. I will scatter you among the nations and draw out a sword after you; your land shall be desolate and your cities waste."

God says He will dwell with His people as long as they are faithful, but when they turn from God, God would become their greatest enemy. Indeed, God used the nations around Israel to administer God's judgment against them time and time again.

God is very patient. The book of Judges shows over and over again the Children of Israel turning their backs on God. God in His love and mercy would make provision for His people and allow them to return to Him.

David Desired To Build A House For God To Dwell

By the time David had secured the throne and was firmly placed in power, he lived in a house of cedar. The land had been taken and the people were settled. David realized that he was living in a fine home but that God was still dwelling in a tent (tabernacle). David desired to build a house for God, but was refused permission by God because David was a man of blood (1 Chronicles 22:8). He did, however, allow

David's son, Solomon, to build the temple (1 Chronicles 22:9-10).

The Building of the Temple As A Dwelling Place for God

Although David was not allowed to build the temple, his son, Solomon, was allowed to build it. God spoke to Solomon and reaffirmed his commitment to dwell with His people. God said, "Concerning this temple which you are building, if you walk in My statutes, execute My judgments, keep all My commandments, and walk in them, then I will perform My word with you, which I spoke to your father David. And I will dwell among the children of Israel, and will not forsake My people Israel" (I King 6:11-13).

The Bible tells of God's move from the tabernacle to the temple. "And it came to pass, when the priests came out of the holy place that the cloud filled the house of the LORD, so that the priests could not continue ministering because of the cloud; for the glory of the LORD filled the house of the LORD. Then Solomon spoke: "The LORD said He would dwell in the dark cloud. I have surely built You an exalted house, and a place for You to dwell in forever" (1 Kings 8:10-13).

God Grows Weary Of His People

After Solomon's reign, God's people went downhill spiritually and turned their backs on God. The glory that was Solomon's was to be no more. After Solomon, the kingdom was divided. The ten northern tribes were eventually carried into Assyrian captivity. Later, Jerusalem and the temple were destroyed and the nation of Judah was carried away into Babylonian captivity by King Nebuchadnezzar.

As the Children of Israel continued to turn from God, God determined that it was time for Him to depart from His people. Ezekiel tells of the presence of God leaving the temple and returning to heaven. "Then the glory of the LORD went up from the cherub, and paused over the threshold of the temple; and the house was filled with the cloud, and the court was full of the brightness of the LORD'S glory" (Ezekiel 10:4). "Then the glory of the LORD departed from the threshold of the temple and stood over the cherubim" (Ezekiel 10:18).

It appears that God gave up on His plan to dwell with man, but God renewed His promise to dwell with him. "Then they shall dwell in the land that I have given to Jacob My servant, where your fathers dwelt; and they shall dwell there, they, their children, and their children's children, forever; and My servant David shall be their prince forever. 'Moreover I will make a covenant of peace with them, and it shall be an everlasting covenant with them; I will establish them and multiply them, and I will set My sanctuary in their midst forevermore. My tabernacle also shall be with them; indeed I will be their God, and they shall be My people. The nations also will know that I, the LORD, sanctify Israel, when My sanctuary is in their midst forevermore'" (Ezekiel 37:25-28).

This prophecy of Ezekiel is one of great importance to us today because it foretells of a new order in which God will dwell with man. This prophecy is fulfilled in the New Testament, the covenant that will continue until the end of time.

The New Testament Reveals Another Plan
For God To Dwell With Man

The New Testament begins with a new plan for God to dwell with man. This time Jesus comes to the earth in the form of a man and dwells with man. In Matthew, chapter one, we see the significance of this when we read in verse 22 and 23, "So all this was done that it might be fulfilled which was spoken by the Lord through the prophet, saying: 'Behold, the virgin shall be with child, and bear a Son, and they shall call His name Immanuel,' which is translated, 'God with us.'" The very name, Immanuel, means God with us. God again demonstrates His desire to dwell with man. Certainly this shows us that we are "Special to God." Again, in the gospel of John we find a similar reading. "And the Word became flesh and dwelt among us, and we beheld His glory, the glory as of the only begotten of the Father, full of grace and truth" (John 1:14).

The Church Was Established That We Might
Dwell With Him

Without a doubt, the Bible teaches that God dwells with man today in the Church. The language of the New Testament shows that God is our Father; that we are members of God's family, and God's household. These are metaphors of this spiritual relationship we have with God. Notice the words of the apostle Paul: "For through Him we both have access by one Spirit to the Father. Now, therefore, you are no longer strangers and foreigners, but fellow citizens with the saints and members of the household of God, having been built on the foundation of the apostles and prophets, Jesus Christ Himself being the chief cornerstone, in whom the whole building, being joined together, grows into a holy temple in the Lord, in whom you also are being built together for a dwelling place of God in the Spirit" (Ephesians 2:18-22).

Just as God dwelt in a physical temple during the Jewish dispensation, in the Christian dispensation He dwells in our hearts when our hearts are right with God. "For you are the temple of the living God. As God has said: 'I will dwell in them and walk among them. I will be their God, and they shall be My people'" (2 Corinthians 6:16). God is in the assembly of the Church when they come together to worship Him. "For where two or three are gathered together in My name, I am there in the midst of them" (Matthew 18:20).

God's Eternal Dwelling

God has never lost His desire to dwell with His people. He plans to live with them eternally. God will dwell with man in the Church and throughout all eternity with those who are saved. "And I heard a loud voice from heaven saying, "Behold, the tabernacle of God is with men, and He will dwell with them, and they shall be His people. God Himself will be with them and be their God. "And God will wipe away every tear from their eyes; there shall be no more death, nor sorrow, nor crying. There shall be no more pain, for the former things have passed away" (Revelation 21:3-4).

While we are on earth, God's dwelling with us is still conditional. He might pull up stakes as He did in the Old Testament during the days of Ezekiel. The condition of God dwelling with us today is our faithful service to Him. If we fail in this, God will keep His promise of not dwelling with the unfaithful. However, when this life is over our fate is sealed. We will spend eternity dwelling with God or spend eternity dwelling apart from God. Those that have lived faithful lives to God will receive the glorious invitation of

God to dwell with Him throughout all eternity. What a joy it will be to hear the words of the Master as was heard by the faithful servants in the Parable of the Talents—"His lord said to him, 'Well *done,* good and faithful servant; you were faithful over a few things, I will make you ruler over many things. Enter into the joy of your lord'" (Matthew 25:21).

Conclusion

Can there be any doubt in your mind that you are "Special to God" after seeing that the Jehovah God of Heaven, the El Shaddai (the God Almighty), thinks that you are so important that He allowed His Son to die for you so you could live with Him. Never, never forget that you are, indeed, "Special to God."

Chapter 3

You Are Special to God Because He Wants You to Talk to Him

"Let us therefore come boldly to the throne of grace, that we may obtain mercy and find grace to help in time of need."

Hebrews 4:16

The God of heaven has always desired to have an open dialogue with His creation. God does not appear to us today in some miraculous manifestation so that we might communicate together, but nevertheless, God communicates to us through His word—The Holy Bible, and God wants us to talk to Him in prayer.

The concept of prayer differs just as people differ. For some, the concept of prayer is "like a Visa card." Just run it through (or by God) and you can have anything you want. Others have the "fire department" concept of God. That is, when there is an emergency in your life, you call on Him. Still others have the view that God will perform miracles for them to bring about the request of the prayer.

I believe that God answers prayers today. But there is much we need to learn about the subject of prayer. In this lesson on talking with God, we want to develop a better understanding of the subject of prayer from a biblical, rather than an emotional, perspective.

The disciples of Jesus recognized the importance of prayer. The scriptures never mention them asking Jesus to teach them how to preach, but they did ask Him to teach them to pray. The Bible says, "Now it came to pass, as He was praying in a certain place, when He ceased, that one of His disciples said to Him, "Lord, teach us to pray, as John also taught his disciples" (Luke 11:1). Jesus answered the disciples by giving them a prayer model. So He said to them, "When you pray, say: 'Our Father in heaven, Hallowed be Your name. Your kingdom come, Your will be done on earth as it is in heaven. Give us day by day our daily bread. And forgive us our sins, for we also forgive everyone who is indebted to us. And do not lead us into temptation, but deliver us from the evil one'" (Luke 11:2-4).

Jesus was a man of prayer. It seems that Jesus was constantly praying, many times slipping away privately to spend time talking to His Heavenly Father. Some of the times we see Jesus praying are: Following his baptism (Luke 3:21); before selecting the twelve (Luke 6:12); before His arrest (John 17:20-21); and while on the cross (Luke 23:34). Other times of prayer were when Jesus simply wanted to be alone in a quiet place to pray. In fact, we are told He looked for a quiet place to pray (Matthew 14:23 and Mark 1:35). He often withdrew Himself to pray (Luke 5:16; Luke 9:18). It seems that Jesus loved to be alone in prayer.

Jesus taught His disciples that God wants to answer our prayers. Notice this passage: "So I say to you, ask, and it will be given to you; seek, and you will find; knock, and it will be opened to you. For everyone who asks receives, and he who seeks finds, and to him who knocks it will be opened. If a son asks for bread from any father among you, will he give him a stone? Or if [he asks] for a fish, will he give him a serpent instead of a fish? Or if he asks for an egg, will he offer him a scorpion? If you then, being evil, know how to give good gifts to your children, how much more will [your] heavenly Father give the Holy Spirit to those who ask Him" (Luke 11:9-13)!

For What Should We Pray?

Now let us look at some biblical examples of things for which we are to pray. We begin by looking at the example prayer that Jesus gave to His disciples: "In this manner, therefore, pray: Our Father in heaven, Hallowed be Your name. Your kingdom come. Your will be done on earth as it is in heaven. Give us this day our daily bread. And forgive us our debts, as we forgive our debtors. And do not lead us into temptation, but deliver us from the evil one. For Yours is the kingdom and the power and the glory forever. Amen" (Matthew 6:9-13).

In this prayer, we find: praise of God; thankfulness for food; forgiveness of sins; that we be not led into temptation; and that we be delivered from Satan. Notice the prayer begins and ends with praise to God. But let us now look at some other things for which we should pray.

We are to pray for our enemies. "But I say to you, love your enemies, bless those who curse you, do good to those who hate you, and pray for those who spitefully use you and persecute you" (Matthew 5:44).

We are to pray for laborers in the gospel. "Then He said to His disciples, 'The harvest truly is plentiful, but the laborers are few. Therefore pray the Lord of the harvest to send out laborers into His harvest'" (Matthew 9:37-38).

We are to pray for safety. Jesus, in predicting the fall of Jerusalem, said, "And pray that your flight may not be in winter or on the Sabbath" (Matthew 24:20).

We are to pray in times of temptation and before temptations. "Watch and pray, lest you enter into temptation. The spirit indeed is willing, but the flesh is weak" (Matthew 26:41).

We are to pray in times of difficulty. "Again, a second time, He went away and prayed, saying, 'O My Father, if this cup cannot pass away from Me unless I drink it, Your will be done' (Matthew 26:42). "So He left them, went away again, and prayed the third time, saying the same words" (Matthew 26:44).

We are to pray that our faith will not fail. "And the Lord said, "Simon, Simon! Indeed, Satan has asked for you, that he may sift you as wheat. But I have prayed for you, that your faith should not fail; and when you have returned to Me, strengthen your brethren" (Luke 22:31-32).

We are to pray in times of decision. "And they proposed two: Joseph called Barsabas, who was surnamed Justus, and Matthias. And they prayed and said, You, O Lord, who know the hearts of all, show which of these two You have chosen" (Acts 1:23-24).

We are to pray for forgiveness. "Repent therefore of this your wickedness, and pray God if perhaps the thought of your heart may be forgiven you" (Acts 8:22). "Then Simon answered and said, "Pray to the Lord for me, that none of the things which you have spoken may come upon me" (Acts 8:24).

We are to pray in times of illness. "Is anyone among you suffering? Let him pray. Is anyone cheerful? Let him sing psalms. Is anyone among you sick? Let him call for the elders of the church, and let them pray over him, anointing him with oil in the name of the Lord. And the prayer of faith will save the sick, and the Lord will raise him up. And if he has committed sins, he will be forgiven" (James 5:13-15).

We are to pray that love might continue. "And this I pray, that your love may abound still more and more in knowledge and all discernment, that you may approve the things that are excellent, that you may be sincere and without offense till the day of Christ, being filled with the fruits of righteousness which are by Jesus Christ, to the glory and praise of God" (Philippians 1:9-11).

We are to pray for the spreading of the gospel. "Continue earnestly in prayer, being vigilant in it with thanksgiving; meanwhile praying also for us, that God would open to us a door for the word, to speak the mystery of Christ, for which I am also in chains" (Colossians 4:2-3).

We are to pray for wisdom. "If any of you lacks wisdom, let him ask of God, who gives to all liberally and without reproach, and it will be given to him. But let him ask in faith, with no doubting, for he who doubts is like a wave of the sea driven and tossed by the wind. For let not that man suppose that he will receive anything from the Lord; he is a double-minded man, unstable in all his ways" (James 1:5-8).

We are to pray for all men. "Therefore I exhort first of all that supplications, prayers, intercessions, *and* giving of thanks be made *for all men*, for kings and all who are in authority, that we may lead a quiet and peaceable life in all godliness and reverence. For this *is* good and acceptable in the sight of God our Savior" (1 Timothy 2:1-3).

And, when we don't know how or what to pray for, we have help (intercession) from the Holy Spirit. "Likewise the Spirit also helps in our weaknesses. For we do not know what we should pray for as we ought, but the Spirit Himself makes intercession for us with groanings which cannot be uttered" (Romans 8:26). The word intercession means, "to make petition; plead with; seeking the presence and hearing of God on behalf of others."

How Should We Pray?

This was a question that the disciples asked Jesus (Luke 11:1). A part of the answer to that question was stated in Matthew's account, where Jesus mentions how not to pray. Jesus warned about praying hypocritically—standing in the synagogues or busy street corners so they could be seen by others. Jesus pointed out the importance of private prayers, even as He said, "Go into your room, and when you have shut your door, pray to your Father." Jesus was also aware of those of His day who repeated phrases. Jesus called them "vain repetitions" and told them not to use them. All of these points are made by Jesus in Matthew 6:5-7. Please take the time to read these verses.

There are many other verses in the Bible that tell us about prayer and how we are to pray. Please notice the following passages.

We are to pray persistently. In the parable found in Luke 18:1-6, Jesus spoke a parable to them, that men always ought to pray and not lose heart. The parable tells of a judge who did not fear God nor regard man. Jesus said there was a widow in that city; and she came to him, saying, "Get justice for me from my adversary. And he would not for a while; but afterward he said within himself, Though I do not fear God nor regard man, yet because this widow troubles me I will avenge her, lest by her continual coming she weary me." Sometimes people offer up a prayer and forget it. It may be that God is interested in hearing from us repeatedly, or we may change His mind by our continued praying.

We are to pray humbly. In Luke 18:10-14, we have the story by Jesus of two men praying. Jesus points out that the prayer of the humble man was accepted, but the prayer of the one who was arrogant, self-righteous, and intent on telling God how good he was, was not accepted. Even though the self-righteous Pharisee was a very religious man (giving tithes and fasting twice each week), his attitude was all wrong. He was condescending toward the humble tax collector. Jesus said that the Pharisee was not justified before God.

We are to pray believing God will answer our prayers. Jesus said, "And whatever things you ask in prayer, believing, you will receive" (Matthew 21:22). And James said, "But let him ask in faith, with no doubting, for he who doubts is like a wave of the sea driven and tossed by the wind. For let not that man suppose that he will receive anything from the Lord; he is a double-minded man, unstable in all his ways" (James 1:6-8).

We are to pray according to God's will. Jesus prayed "Your will be done" (Matthew 26:42). So often when we pray, we want our will to be done, not God's will. John points out that we are to pray according to God's will. He said, "Now this is the confidence that we have in Him, that if we ask anything according to His will, He hears us" (1 John 5:14). God wants us to have blessings and He wants us to ask for them.

We are to pray with confidence and assurance. The Hebrew writer says, "Let us therefore come boldly to the throne of grace, that we may obtain mercy and find grace to help in time of need" (Hebrews 4:16). This doesn't mean that we are to come brashly, demanding that God answer our prayers. It means that we are to have confidence and assurance in our prayers and God's ability to answer them. The Revised Standard Version says, "Let us then with confidence draw near to the throne of grace." As a child of God, we have confidence and assurance that God hears our prayers.

Are All Prayers Acceptable To God?

The Bible teaches that there are conditions of acceptable prayer. Keep in mind that even if we meet these conditions, God may not answer our prayer the way we want it answered. Someone has said that God answers prayers three ways: **(1)** Yes. **(2)** No, and **(3)** Maybe later, or not right now.

We are to be righteous. "For the eyes of the LORD [are] on the righteous, and His ears [are open] to their prayers; but the face of the LORD [is] against those who do evil" (1 Peter 3:12).

We are to keep God's commandments. "And whatever we ask we receive from Him, because we keep His commandments and do those things that are pleasing in His sight" (1 John 3:22). The Holy Spirit places the condition of commandment keeping and being pleasing to God as conditions for receiving blessings from God.

We are to pray in faith. "But let him ask in faith, with no doubting, for he who doubts is like a wave of the sea driven and tossed by the wind. For let not that man suppose that he will receive anything from the Lord" (James 1:6-7).

We are to pray in Jesus' name. "And [whatever] you do in word or deed, [do] all in the name of the Lord Jesus, giving thanks to God the Father through Him" (Colossians 3:17).

We are to pray with a forgiving spirit. "For if you forgive men their trespasses, your heavenly Father will also forgive you. But if you do not forgive men their trespasses, neither will your Father forgive your trespasses" (Matthew 6:14-15).

We are to pray with the right motive in mind. "You ask and do not receive, because you ask amiss, that you may spend [it] on your pleasures" (James 4:3).

We must not abuse prayer. Men abuse prayer by thinking prayer is all that is necessary to please God. In fact, most protestant denominations teach that we are saved by prayer. How often I've heard, "Just accept Christ as your personal Savior, and pray the sinner's prayer." The problem with this is that nowhere in the Bible can one find the passage that teaches that an alien sinner is saved by prayer!

We can also abuse prayer by praying to be seen of men. Jesus warns about hypocritical prayer when He said, "And when you pray, you shall not be like the hypocrites. For they love to pray standing in the synagogues and on the corners of the streets, that they may be seen by men. Assuredly, I say to you, they have their reward. But you, when you pray, go into your room, and when you have shut your door, pray to your Father who [is] in the secret [place;] and your Father who sees in secret will reward you openly.

And when you pray, do not use vain repetitions as the heathen [do.] For they think that they will be heard for their many words. Therefore do not be like them. For your Father knows the things you have need of before you ask Him" (Matthew 6:5-8).

Our prayers should be without hypocrisy. As mentioned in the previous passage; Jesus condemned those who stood in the synagogues and street corners, praying to be heard of men. Jesus points out that their reward is that others see them pray. This obviously means God does not answer their prayers.

We are to pray without ceasing. "Pray without ceasing, in everything give thanks; for this is the will of God in Christ Jesus for you" (1 Thessalonians 5:17-18). This simply means that we are to be constant and consistent in prayer. It also teaches that we are to give thanks to God. How often do we pray for things and then fail to thank God for the blessing we receive?

We are to pray without wavering. "If any of you lacks wisdom, let him ask of God, who gives to all liberally and without reproach, and it will be given to him. But let him ask in faith, with no doubting, for he who doubts is like a wave of the sea driven and tossed by the wind. For let not that man suppose that he will receive anything from the Lord; [he is] a double-minded man, unstable in all his ways" (James 1:5-8). A lack of faith is a "prayer killer" if there ever was one.

We are not to be self-righteous. Such was the Pharisee in the account of Luke. "Two men went up to the temple to pray, one a Pharisee and the other a tax collector. The Pharisee stood and prayed thus with himself, 'God, I thank

You that I am not like other men, extortioners, unjust, adulterers, or even as this tax collector. I fast twice a week; I give tithes of all that I possess. And the tax collector, standing afar off, would not so much as raise [his] eyes to heaven, but beat his breast, saying, God, be merciful to me a sinner! I tell you, this man went down to his house justified [rather] than the other; for everyone who exalts himself will be humbled, and he who humbles himself will be exalted" (Luke 18:10-14).

We are not to use vain repetitions. Jesus said, "And when you pray, do not use vain repetitions as the heathen [do.] For they think that they will be heard for their many words" (Matthew 6:7). The Revised Standard Version says, "And in praying do not heap up empty phrases as the Gentiles do; for they think that they will be heard for their many words." Albert Barnes says of this passage that vain repetitions "means to repeat a thing often, to say the same thing in different words, or to repeat the same words, as though God did not hear at first."

Conclusion

How wonderful it is to worship the God of heaven; the One who loves me and wants me to talk with Him, giving my adoration to Him and being able to confess to Him my faults and find forgiveness of sins. Our God is an awesome God, and we are, indeed, "Special to God."

Chapter 4

You Are Special to God Because He Wants You to Hear Him

"While he was still speaking, behold, a bright cloud overshadowed them; and suddenly a voice came out of the cloud, saying, 'This is My beloved Son, in whom I am well pleased. Hear Him.'"

Matthew 17:5

As stated previously, the God of heaven has desired to have an open dialogue with His creation since the beginning of time. From the Garden of Eden to the present day, God speaks to man. God does not appear to us today in some miraculous manifestation so that we might communicate together, but nevertheless, God speaks to us through the Bible, His word to man. Our attitude toward Bible study should be that as we read, God is speaking to us. Our desire for God's word should be a desire to feed the spiritual man just as we eat to feed our physical bodies. We read that God's word is compared to milk for newborn babes (spiritually) and that we should desire it that we may grow spiritually (I Peter 2:2). The things difficult to understand in God's word are referred to as strong meat, and in order to grow spiritually, we are to desire this meat (Hebrews 5:12-14).

In the book of Hebrews, we read that "God, who at various times and in various ways spoke in time past to the fathers by the prophets, has in these last days spoken to us by His Son, whom He has appointed heir of all things, through whom also He made the worlds" (Hebrews 1:1-2). So we see that God has always communicated His will to man, whether by speaking to the patriarchs, or through the Law of Moses, or through His prophets. But lastly, God spoke to man through His Son Jesus Christ.

Our attitude in hearing what God has to say to us should be the same as the attitude of the prophet Samuel. When God spoke to Samuel, he responded to God by saying, "Speak, for Your servant hears" (1 Samuel 3:10). Our world would be better off spiritually if we all had this attitude. When God speaks, we should desire to hear what He has to say to us and then follow His will in our lives so that we might be pleasing to Him.

We Must Hear The Lord

The word of God, when spoken to man, is for man's benefit. When Jesus was on the Mount of Transfiguration with Peter, James, and John as witnesses to the Lord's appearance with Moses and Elijah, the Bible says, "While he was still speaking, behold, a bright cloud overshadowed them; and suddenly a voice came out of the cloud, saying, 'This is My beloved Son, in whom I am well pleased. Hear Him'" (Matthew 17:5)!

In Acts 3:22-23, Peter, speaking to the Jews, said, "For Moses truly said to the fathers, 'The LORD your God will raise up for you a Prophet like me from your brethren. Him you shall hear in all things, whatever He says to you. And it shall be that every soul who will not hear that Prophet shall be utterly destroyed from among the people.'"

Hearing The Lord Is To Hear His Word

If we hear the word of the Lord and trust in Him, we can have salvation. In Ephesians 1:13, Paul says, **"In Him *you* also trusted, after you heard the word of truth,** the gospel of your salvation; in whom also, having believed, you were sealed with the Holy Spirit of promise." In Colossians 1:5, Paul tells of the hope we have in heaven as a result of hearing the gospel. He says, "because of the hope which is laid up for you in heaven, of which you heard before in the word of the truth of the gospel."

The importance of hearing the word of God is stressed by none other than The Christ, when he said, "Most assuredly, I say to you, he who hears My word and believes in Him who sent Me has everlasting life, and shall not come into judgment, but has passed from death into life. Most assuredly, I say to you, the hour is coming, and now is, when the dead will hear the voice of the Son of God; and those who hear will live" (John 5:24-25).

Hearing His Word Will Produce Faith

Paul asked the question, "How shall they believe in Him of whom they have not heard?" (Romans 10:14). We are told in the scriptures that "faith comes by hearing, and hearing by the word of God" (Romans 10:17), and that "without faith it is impossible to please Him, for he who comes to God must believe that He is, and that He is a rewarder of those who diligently seek Him" (Hebrews 11:6).

Those who hear the word and refuse to allow the word into their hearts and to change them into what God desires will not be profited by the word of God. "For indeed the gospel was preached to us as well as to them; but the word which they heard did not profit them, not being mixed with faith in those who heard it" (Hebrews 4:2). The Proverbs writer says that the "one who turns away his ear from hearing the law, even his prayer is an abomination" (Proverbs 28:9).

We Are To Hear In the Assembly

"Walk prudently when you go to the house of God; and draw near to hear rather than to give the sacrifice of fools, for they do not know that they do evil" (Ecclesiastes 5:1). It was the hearing of God's word that cut the heart of those Jews on Pentecost and caused them to come to Christ. "Now when they heard *this,* they were cut to the heart, and said to Peter and the rest of the apostles, 'Men *and* brethren, what shall we do?' Then Peter said to them, 'Repent, and let every one of you be baptized in the name of Jesus Christ for the remission of sins; and you shall receive the gift of the Holy Spirit. For the promise is to you and to your children, and to all who are afar off, as many as the Lord our God will call'" (Acts 2:37-39).

Inspiration records for us the story of a man who went to sleep in the worship services and fell from a third story window and died. (Paul raised the dead man.) We are told about this man in Acts 20:7-10. The man's name was Eutychus. What a way to be remembered for 2,000 years!

Why Do Some Not Listen?

The reasons for not listening, especially in the assembly, are varied. But whatever the reason, or excuse, for not listening to God's message, we still are obligated to hear God! Some of the reasons given for not listening are:

- Boring speaker
- Indifference
- Physical reasons
- Trained to sleep in worship
- Environment
- Distractions caused by others
- Concerns about issues facing them
- Dissatisfaction with the worship service
- Worship weariness

What Can The Listener Do To Improve Hearing?

Many times listening can be improved by taking simple precautions to focus one's attention on the subject at hand. Consider the following to improve attention during worship services:

- Take notes.
- Follow along in your Bible.
- Make a personal application to the scripture.
- Study before hand. Prepare.
- Pray.
- Bring your Bible to worship and use it.

Dull Hearing Hinders Spiritual Reasoning and Discernment

The Hebrews writer speaks of those who have become dull of hearing and points out the need for spiritual growth and development. "Of whom we have much to say, and hard to explain, *since you have become dull of hearing.* For though by this time you ought to be teachers, you need someone to teach you again the first principles of the oracles of God; and you have come to need milk and not solid food. For everyone who partakes only of milk is unskilled in the word of righteousness, for he is a babe. But solid food belongs to those who are of full age, that is, those who by reason of use have their senses exercised to discern both good and evil" (Hebrews 5:11-14).

Hearing without Doing Is Of Little Value

We cannot be justified before God if we do not hear His word. Paul said, "For not the hearers of the law are just in the sight of God, but the doers of the law will be justified" (Romans 2:13).

Hearing Without Doing Is Deception To Oneself

Sometimes we deceive ourselves into thinking that hearing God is all that is necessary on the part of the Christian. This is not true. The Bible teaches that we are to "Be doers of the word, and not hearers only, deceiving yourselves." That to hear God's word and not do what he says is like one "observing his natural face in a mirror; for he observes himself, goes away, and immediately forgets what kind of man he was. But he who looks into the perfect law of liberty and continues *in it,* and is not a forgetful hearer but **a doer of the work**, this one will be blessed in what he does" (James 1:22-25).

A Wise Man Is One Who Hears The Word Of God And Obeys

Jesus pointed out that the one that enters the kingdom of heaven is the one who not only hears God's will for man, but the one who does God's will. "Not everyone who says to Me, 'Lord, Lord,' shall enter the kingdom of heaven, but he who does the will of My Father in heaven. Many will say to Me in that day, 'Lord, Lord, have we not prophesied in Your name, cast out demons in Your name, and done many wonders in Your name?' And then I will declare to them, 'I never knew you; depart from Me, you who practice lawlessness'" (Matthew 7:21-23)! Jesus goes on to say in this passage that one who hears God's words and does not do them is "like a foolish man who built his house on the sand: and the rain descended, the floods came, and the winds blew and beat on that house; and it fell. And great was its fall" (Matthew 7:26-27).

Jesus said the wise man builds his house on the rock. He likens the wise man as to one who hears God's word, then does what God says. When the storms came, the wise man's house stood firm. It is a wise person, indeed, who will hear God's word and then make a determination to do what God says, regardless of the consequences. This may involve the breaking of ties with others, even family members that would oppose your serving Jesus Christ.

Take Heed How We Hear And What We Hear

What we hear and how we hear are important to Jesus. He tells us this in two verses of scripture.

55

Luke 8:18 "Therefore **take heed how you hear**. For whoever has, to him [more] will be given; and whoever does not have, even what he seems to have will be taken from him."

Mark 4:24 "Then He said to them, **'Take heed what you hear.** With the same measure you use, it will be measured to you; and to you who hear, more will be given.'"

With this in mind, let us look at some ways that we are to hear and what we must hear.

We need to hear attentively. In Nehemiah, chapter 8, after Nehemiah had led the Jews in rebuilding the walls of Jerusalem, the people were assembled and Ezra read the Law of God in their hearing. This was not a thirty minute sermonette. The reading lasted from morning to noon each day for seven days. We are told, "Then he (Ezra-FR) read from it in the open square that [was] in front of the Water Gate from morning until midday, before the men and women and those who could understand; **and the ears of all the people were attentive** to the Book of the Law." In the New Testament, when Jesus drove the money changers out of the temple, the Jewish leaders sought to destroy Him, but "were unable to do anything; **for all the people were very attentive to hear Him"** (Luke 19:48).

We need to hear reverently. So often this is not the case. The word, "reverent", means to revere or hold in great honor the one speaking. When God speaks to us, we must listen reverently as the household of Cornelius did in Acts 10:33 when Peter came to speak to them the words of the Lord. Cornelius said, "...Now therefore, we are all present before God, **to hear all the things commanded you by God."**

We need to hear honestly. By this, we mean that people should honestly strive to follow the words of the Lord. As Samuel said, "Speak, for your servant hears" (1 Samuel 3:10). When God speaks to us through His word, will we be honest with ourselves in believing and accepting what God says, regardless of what others may say? Some may think you have "lost it." Others may think you are "brainwashed." But hearing honestly and determining to do what our Lord desires are the most important decisions one will ever make.

We need to hear inquiringly. Personal honesty requires that we test the things we hear from people claiming to be religious teachers. This is done in light of truth. Jesus said, "Sanctify them by your truth; Your word is truth" (John 17:17).

We need to hear personally. So often, the application of God's word completely misses us as we fail to see ourselves in what is being said. This was true of King David when Nathan told the story of the rich man taking the poor man's pet lamb and killing it and feeding it to a guest. David was irate, demanding the death of the one who would do such a thing. Nathan had to make the personal application for David by saying, "You are the man" (2 Samuel 12:7). David had taken the wife of Uriah the Hittite, committed adultery with her, and then tried to cover it up. When he could not cover his sin, he had Uriah put to death.

We need to hear obediently. In James 1:21-25, James points out that one who hears God's word and does not follow that word by changing his or her life, is like a person looking in a mirror and later forgetting what he or she looks like. When we look into the Bible, we see what we ought to be. If we refuse to do what we should do, we are like the one that forgets what he or she looks like.

Conclusion

Many times it is difficult for us to hear. We think five times faster than we hear. For this reason, often our minds wander, and we pay less attention to what we should be hearing. However, we still must hear what God has to say to man. God speaks to us through His word, the Holy Bible. We should make a habit of reading and heeding the scriptures. They can shape our lives into something better than we were before we accepted the saving power of the gospel of Christ. Let's all make a point to improve our hearing.

Isn't it wonderful that we worship a God that wants to speak to us and provide us with great spiritual blessings? Truly, we are "Special to God!"

Chapter 5

You Are Special to God Because He Provides For You

"I have been young, and now am old; yet I have not seen the righteous forsaken or his children begging bread."

Psalms 37:25

We can know that we are special to God because of the promises that God has given us that He will take care of us. God takes care of us today through His providence. Providence is defined as the preservation, care, and government which God exercises over all things that He has created in order that they may accomplish the ends for which they were created. Providence differs from miracles in that its ends are brought about by means of the established laws of God and through ordinary channels.

Many people today have a great desire to attribute many good things to miracles. A miracle is defined as an act of God superseding or suspending a natural law. The Bible teaches that miracles have ceased (1 Corinthains 13:8-13) and do not exist today. Miracles were used during the first century to "confirm the word" (Mark 16:20). Once the inspired New Testament was complete, then miracles ceased. However, many attest or claim witness to miracles today. However, most people will tell you they have never seen a miracle. And while many are waiting on miracles to solve their particular situation, God's providence is sustaining them. We need to learn that God does not need to use miracles in the lives of people today to bring about the result that He desires. We tend to forget that in Jesus' example of prayer, He said, "Your will be done" (Matthew 6:10). Before His death, He prayed saying, "Father, if it is Your will, take this cup away from Me; nevertheless not My will, but Yours, be done" (Luke 22:42). We need to remember as we pray, to pray for God's will to be done in all things.

The Scriptures Prove That God Will Provide for His People

Jesus, in the Sermon on the Mount, used this opportunity to point out that people worry needlessly. Notice in this passage what Jesus says about God's providential care.

> "Therefore I say to you, do not worry about your life, what you will eat or what you will drink; nor about your body, what you will put on. Is not life more than food and the body more than clothing? Look at the birds of the air, for they neither sow nor reap nor gather into barns; yet your heavenly Father feeds them. Are you not of more value than they? Which of you by worrying can add one cubit to his stature?"
>
> "So why do you worry about clothing? Consider the lilies of the field, how they grow: they neither toil nor spin; and yet I say to you that even Solomon in all his

glory was not arrayed like one of these. Now if God so clothes the grass of the field, which today is, and tomorrow is thrown into the oven, will He not much more clothe you, O you of little faith? Therefore do not worry, saying, 'What shall we eat?' or 'What shall we drink?' or 'What shall we wear?' For after all these things the Gentiles seek. For your heavenly Father knows that you need all these things. But seek first the kingdom of God and His righteousness, and all these things shall be added to you. Therefore do not worry about tomorrow, for tomorrow will worry about its own things. Sufficient for the day is its own trouble." (Matthew 6:25-34).

The message is clear—don't worry! Why? Because God will take care of His people! We are so much like the people of the first century. Two thousand years later, we, like them, worry about what we are going to eat, what we are going to drink, and what we are going to wear. We worry about our life. Some even worry about their height. Jesus says don't worry about these things. "Therefore do not worry, saying, 'What shall we eat?' or 'What shall we drink?' or 'What shall we wear'" (Matthew 6:31).

Our Lord is so aware of our everyday situations. In Matthew 10:29, He speaks of birds, saying, "Are not two sparrows sold for a copper coin? And not one of them falls to the ground apart from your Father's will." And in Luke 12:7, He says, "But the very hairs of your head are all numbered. Do not fear therefore; you are of more value than many sparrows." Again, the message from God is the same—God cares for you. He knows you so intimately. If God knows the number of hairs on our heads, He knows our needs, wants, desires, sins, dreams, ambitions and aspirations. If God is concerned about a sparrow falling to the ground, the obvious message from inspiration is that God cares for His people, and they are special to God.

Another Bible passage that tells us not to worry is Philippians 4:6. "Be anxious for nothing, but in everything by prayer and supplication, with thanksgiving, let your requests be made known to God." The Modern New Testament translates this passage as, "Do not worry about anything; but in everything by prayer and supplication, with thanksgiving, let your requests be made known to God." Albert Barnes in his Commentary on Philippians says that the word "does not mean that we are to exercise no care about worldly matters—no care to preserve our property, or to provide for our families, (1Timothy 5:8); but that there is to be such confidence in God as to free the mind from anxiety, and such a sense of dependence on Him as to keep it calm."

It is God that gives us rain from heaven to sustain life; along with fruitful seasons so we might have food to eat (Acts 14:17). The psalmist said, "Who covers the heavens with clouds, who prepares rain for the earth, who makes grass to grow on the mountains. He gives to the beast its food, and to the young ravens that cry" (Psalm 147:8-9).

Speaking of God's preservation of His people, Nehemiah said, "You alone are the LORD; you have made heaven, the heaven of heavens, with all their host, the earth and everything on it, the seas and all that is in them, and **You preserve them all.** The host of heaven worships You" (Nehemiah 9:6).

The writer of the Book of Hebrews tells us that God has given us a promise of His providence when he stated, "For He Himself has said, 'I will never leave you nor forsake you'" (Hebrews 13:5).

Providence In The Life Of Moses

Moses was born the son of Hebrew slaves during a time that the Pharaoh had proclaimed that all newborn male babies of the Hebrews were to be put to death. Moses' mother hid the child in a basket and put the basket in the Nile River near a place where Pharaoh's daughter came to bathe. Pharaoh's daughter saw the baby and desired to have the baby as her own. Moses' sister, who was watching nearby, asked if she could find a nurse for the baby. When told yes, she went to her mother and told her what had happened and Moses' mother became his nurse.

Moses grew up in Pharaoh's house and became an important member of the ruling family of Egypt. However, upon learning of his Hebrew heritage, he forsook the ruling family to become a Hebrew slave. The Hebrew writer tells us, "By faith Moses, when he became of age, refused to be called the son of Pharaoh's daughter, choosing rather to suffer affliction with the people of God than to enjoy the passing pleasures of sin, esteeming the reproach of Christ greater riches than the treasures in Egypt; for he looked to the reward. By faith he forsook Egypt, not fearing the wrath of the king; for he endured as seeing Him who is invisible" (Hebrews 11:24-27).

This same Moses, who was exiled from Egypt, returned when he was eighty years old to lead the children of Israel out of Egyptian bondage. All of this was done by the providence of God. Yes, God used miracles to bring Egypt to her knees and grant the release of the Hebrews, but God's providence brought Moses to this point in his life.

Providence In The Life Of Joseph

The story of Joseph is one of the greatest stories ever recorded. Because he revealed the dreams that he had concerning his brothers bowing down to him, and because his father, Jacob, showed favoritism to him, Joseph's brothers decided to kill him. At the last minute, they decided to sell him as a slave, and he was carried to Egypt where he served in the house of Potiphar. When Potiphar's wife made sexual advances toward Joseph, he refused. This resulted in trumped up charges of misconduct against Joseph and he was thrown into prison.

While in prison, Joseph interpreted the dreams of a butler and a baker. Joseph interpreted the butler's dream, telling him that he would be restored to his position. Two years went by and the pharaoh had a dream. The butler told him that Joseph could interpret dreams. Joseph was called before the pharaoh and correctly interpreted the pharaoh's dream to mean that Egypt would have seven years of plenty followed by seven years of famine. The pharaoh made Joseph the second in command over all of Egypt.

Years passed, and Jacob sent his sons (with the exception of Benjamin) to Egypt to buy grain. When they arrived in Egypt at the place of the grain sale, Joseph was there and recognized his brothers. Eventually, he made himself known to his brothers. Later, his father and the rest of the family came to Egypt under the protection of the pharaoh. When Jacob died, Joseph's brothers thought that Joseph would now bring on them retribution for their actions against him many years before. Instead, Joseph said, "Do not be afraid, for am I in the place of God? "But as for you, you meant evil against me; but God meant it for good, in order to bring it about as it is this day, to save many people alive. God sent me before you to preserve life" (Genesis 45:19-20).

God brought about the salvation of the young Hebrew nation from starvation, not by any miracle, but through His providence—through His preservation, care, and government brought about by means of His established laws and through ordinary channels. God preserved an entire nation, not by miracles, but by His providence.

Providence In The Life Of Esther

Esther, a Jew, was married to Ahasuerus, king of Persia, the most powerful man in the world at that time. He is known in the history books as Xerxes, the king of Persia that tried to conquer Greece in 480 B. C. When Haman, the chief advisor to Ahasuerus, became angry at Mordecai, Esther's cousin, for not bowing to him, Haman determined to destroy all the Jews in the land. In the meantime, Mordecai uncovered a plot against the king and made it known. Those involved in the plot were arrested and killed. This action was rewarded by the king.

Haman's hatred for Mordecai was so great, he built great gallows on which to hang him. After Haman had succeeded in getting a law passed to eradicate the Jews, Esther intervened. She risked her own life by going before the king. When the treachery of Haman was made known, the king had Haman hung on his own gallows, and the lives of the Jews were spared. All of this took place as a result of God's providence—God's care and protection of His people.

God Answers Our Prayers through Providence

Does God answer prayers? I believe He does. He answers prayers by His providence. Perhaps sometimes, we question whether God has the power to grant our petitions. "For the eyes of the Lord are on the righteous, and His ears are open to their prayers; but the face of the Lord is against those who do evil" (1 Peter 3:12).

God wants us to seek Him in prayer. Not only does God want us to seek Him in prayer, He wants to answer our prayers. God liberally gives His blessings to His people.

James said, "If any of you lacks wisdom, let him ask of God, who gives to all liberally and without reproach, and it will be given to him. But let him ask in faith, with no doubting, for he who doubts is like a wave of the sea driven and tossed by the wind. For let not that man suppose that he will receive anything from the Lord" (James 1:5-7).

The Bible mentions a number of things for which we should pray. Jesus said, "Therefore pray the Lord of the harvest to send out laborers into His harvest" (Matthew 9:38). He also said we should pray for our daily bread, forgiveness of debts, for deliverance from temptation and from the devil (Matthew 6:11-13). Paul says we are to pray that "God would open to us a door for the word" (Colossians 4:3). James says we are to pray for the sick (James 5:14), and Paul says to "pray for all men, for kings and all who are in authority" (1 Timothy 2:12).

Some Instances Of Providence In The Bible

From Nave's Topical Bible, we find a number of things listed as instances of God's providence, God's special care and protection of His people. In looking at these examples, we can gain assurance that God loves and cares for us. As God cared for His people in times past, He cares for us today. We can learn that we are "Special to God." Take your Bible and read the stories of God's preservation of His people.

- Saving Noah, Genesis 7:1.
- The call of Abraham, Genesis 12:1.
- Protecting Abraham and Sarah, Genesis 20:3–6.
- To Hagar, when Abraham cast her out, Genesis 21:17, 19.
- To Jacob, when he fled from Laban, his father-in-law, Genesis 31:24, 29.

- When Jacob met Esau, Genesis 33:3–10.
- As Jacob journeyed in the land of Canaan, Genesis 35:5.
- To Joseph, in Egypt, Genesis 39:2, 21.
- To Moses, in his infancy, Exodus 2:1–10.
- In exempting the land of Goshen from the plague of flies, Exodus 8:22.
- In preserving their cattle from the plague of murrain, Exodus 9:4–7.
- In exempting the land of Goshen from the plague of darkness, Exodus 10:21–23.
- In saving the firstborn, when the plague of death destroyed the firstborn of Egypt, Exodus 12:13, 23.
- Deliverance of Lot, Genesis 19.
- Care of Isaac, Genesis 26:2, 3.
- The mission of Joseph, Genesis 39:2, 3, 23; 45:7, 8; 50:20; Psalms 105:17–22.
- Delivering the Israelites, Exodus 3:8; 11:3; 13:18; Acts 7:34–36.
- Protection of homes while at feasts, Exodus 34:24.
- In the conquest of Canaan, Psalms 44:2, 3.
- Saving David's army, 2 Samuel 5:23–25.
- Fighting the battles of Israel, 2 Chronicles 13:12, 18; 14:9–14; 16:7–9; 20:15, 17, 22, 23; 32:21, 22.
- Restoring Manasseh after his conversion, 2 Chronicles 33:12, 13.
- Feeding Elijah and the widow, 1 Kings 17; 19:1–8.
- In prospering Hezekiah, 2 Kings 18:6,7; 2 Chronicles 32:29.
- Protection of Daniel in the lions' den, Daniel 6.
- In turning the heart of the king of Assyria to favor the Jews, Ezra 6:22.
- In rescuing Jeremiah, Lamentations 3:52–58, with Jeremiah 38:6–13.

- Restoration of the Jews, 2 Chronicles 36:22, 23; Ezra 1:1-4.
- Rescuing the Jews from Haman's plot, the Book of Esther.
- Rebuilding the walls of Jerusalem, Nehemiah 6:16.
- Warning Joseph in dreams, Matthew 1:20; 2:13, 19, 20.
- Warning the wise men of the east, Matthew 2:12, 13.
- Restoring Epaphroditus, Philippians 2:27.
- In the banishment of John to Patmos, Revelation 1:9.

Conclusion

Just as God worked in the lives of Moses, Joseph, and Esther, and scores of other Bible characters, including David, Paul, and Peter, God works in our lives today. His providence and promises are real. We must believe this and take comfort from it.

God promises He will provide for us. We must put our trust and confidence in Him, and believe that He will keep His word to us. Many are waiting for a miracle in their lives and fail to recognize God's everyday care through providence. Isn't it wonderful to know that **"the Lord is my shepherd, I shall not want"** (Psalms 23:1), and that we are "Special to God."

Chapter 6

You Are Special to God Because He Knows How You Feel

"Casting all your care upon Him, for He cares for you"

1 Peter 5:7

"A store owner was tacking a sign above his door that read 'Puppies for Sale.' Signs like that have a way of attracting small children, and sure enough, a little boy appeared under the store owner's sign. 'How much are you going to sell the puppies for?' the little boy asked. The store owner replied, 'anywhere from $30 to $50.' The little boy reached into his pocket and pulled out some change. 'I have $2.37,' he said. 'May I please look at them?' The store owner smiled and whistled and out of the kennel came Lady, who ran down the aisle of his store followed by five teeny, tiny balls of fur."

"One puppy was lagging considerably behind. Immediately the little boy singled out the lagging, limping puppy and said, 'What's wrong with that little dog?' The store owner explained that the veterinarian had examined the little puppy and had discovered that it didn't have a hip socket. It would always limp. It would always be lame. The little boy became excited. 'That is the puppy I want to buy.' The store owner said, 'No, you don't want to buy that little dog. If you really want him, I'll just give him to you.'"

"The little boy got quite upset. He looked straight into the store owner's eyes, pointing his finger, and said, 'I don't want you to give him to me. That little dog is worth every bit as much as all the other dogs and I'll pay full price. In fact, I'll give you $2.37 now and 50 cents a month until I have him paid for.'"

"The store owner countered, 'You really don't want to buy this little dog. He is never going to be able to run and jump and play with you like the other puppies.' To his surprise, the little boy reached down and rolled up his pant leg to reveal a badly twisted, crippled left leg supported by a big metal brace. He looked up at the store owner and softly replied, 'Well, I don't run so well myself, and the little puppy will need someone who understands'" (elsfriend.net).

This story has been told in many ways and in many cultures over the years. The message is such a touching one. The boy knew how the puppy felt because he had suffered from a similar problem. In the same manner, Jesus Christ, the Son of the Living God, knows how we feel because "He has been there."

Jesus was a very caring compassionate man. His love and concern for others caused Him to work to near exhaustion while on the earth. Not only does Jesus care, but He also knows how we feel. Isn't it comforting to know that deity can feel as we feel and care about us when we face the trials of life? Notice what Peter says about our Lord: "Casting all your care upon Him, for **He cares for you**" (1 Peter 5:7).

70

The first word, "care", in this passage means "anxiety" according to W. E. Vine's Expository of New Testament Words. The second word, "care", in this passage is defined by Vine as an object of care, especially the care of forethought and interest. James Strong, in his Strong's Greek Dictionary, says that care means, "it matters."

It does matter to God. It matters to God when we hurt, when we are ill, when the problems and anxieties of this life become so great it seems that we cannot bear it. He knows how we feel.

Jesus Knows How You Feel When Serious Economic Situations Arise

Jesus, while living upon this earth, had very little in the realm of creature comforts. In fact, when told by a potential follower that he would follow Jesus, He replied, "Foxes have holes and birds of the air have nests, but the Son of Man has nowhere to lay His head" (Matthew 8:19-20).

Jesus Knows How You Feel When You Are Falsely Accused and Persecuted

Jesus knew a great deal about persecution. Several times in His ministry, the Jews tried to kill Him, and they succeeded when the time of His ministry came to a close. But notice what Jesus said in the Sermon on the Mount: "Blessed are those who are persecuted for righteousness sake, for theirs is the kingdom of heaven. Blessed are you when they revile and persecute you, and say all kinds of evil against you falsely for My sake. Rejoice and be exceedingly glad, for great *is* your reward in heaven, for so they persecuted the prophets who were before you (Matthew 5:10-12).

When you are falsely accused and persecuted for that which is right and holy—take heart! Jesus suffered for the same things and He will bless those that are persecuted.

Have you ever been falsely accused of things? Have you ever been laughed at or made fun of because of your belief in Jesus Christ? You are not alone. This goes with the territory, so to speak, and you might as well get used to it if you intend to live the life of a Christian. But never forget, Jesus knows what's going on.

Jesus Knows How You Feel When A Friend Betrays You

One of the greatest disappointments of life is for a friend to turn his or her back on you. Perhaps the question in Shakespeare's play, Julius Caesar, "Et tu, Brute?" (You too, Brutus?) hits home with all of us. In the play, Caesar is astonished and hurt that his friend, Brutus, has thrown in with the conspirators to kill him and has taken part in his assassination. While we have not experienced betrayal to this level, we have probably all experienced "character assassination" by one we thought to be our friend. And many times, one who is trying to live a Christian life will find that "so-called friends" are gathering behind your back and betraying you, perhaps in confidences that you thought were safe with them.

Jesus was betrayed by one of His closest companions, Judas Iscariot. "And while He was still speaking, behold, a multitude; and he who was called Judas, one of the twelve, went before them and drew near to Jesus to kiss Him. But Jesus said to him, 'Judas, are you betraying the Son of Man with a kiss'" (Luke 22:47-48)? Yes, Jesus knows what it is like to be betrayed by a friend!

Jesus Knows How You Feel When You Are Rejected Because Of Your Beliefs

It is so common to be rejected when your beliefs differ from the majority. You become the subject of ridicule and scorn. You become the "laughing stock" of the party, the outcast; a fool in the eyes of the majority.

Well, you are in good company if this describes you. Jesus knows exactly how you feel. The Bible says, "He came to His own, and His own did not receive Him. But as many as received Him, to them He gave the right to become children of God, to those who believe in His name" (John 1:11-12).

In the service of Jesus Christ, rejection comes with the territory. If we haven't experienced it yet, get ready! It is coming. Notice what Jesus said of the imminent suffering of His disciples. "From that time Jesus began to show to His disciples that He must go to Jerusalem, and suffer many things from the elders and chief priests and scribes, and be killed, and be raised the third day" (Matthew 16:21).

Many times when you try to do good, others will find fault in you. Such was the case of Jesus after miraculously healing the withered hand of a man. Instead of praising God for this miracle, the "Pharisees went out and plotted against Him, how they might destroy Him" (Matthew 12:14).

Jesus Knows How You Feel When You Are Criticized

Most of us have received our share of criticism, perhaps unjustly. Have you ever tried to do something good and have been accused of having evil motives? Jesus experienced this. Jesus treated everyone equally, while many looked down on those with whom Jesus associated.

73

Notice Matthew 9:10-12: "Now it happened, as Jesus sat at the table in the house, that behold, many tax collectors and sinners came and sat down with Him and His disciples. And when the Pharisees saw *it,* they said to His disciples, "Why does your Teacher eat with tax collectors and sinners?" When Jesus heard *that,* He said to them, "Those who are well have no need of a physician, but those who are sick."

On another occasion, Jesus spoke of the unjust treatment He received. "For John came neither eating nor drinking, and they say, 'He has a demon.' The Son of Man came eating and drinking, and they say, 'Look, a glutton and a winebibber, a friend of tax collectors and sinners!' But wisdom is justified by her children" (Matthew 11:18-19).

Jesus Knows How You Feel When
You Feel Misunderstood

Have you ever dreaded going back to a high school reunion? Many have, and one of the reasons is that when you go back to that setting, you become a kid again, with all the baggage of your teenage years. You have the same insecurities, the same thoughts of acceptance or rejection, and you feel that the person you have become is still the person you were in high school.

You can become one of the most prominent people in your field, attain multiple degrees and accolades from many levels, but when you come back home you are still the freckled-faced boy or the girl with braces on her teeth, and you are treated like that kid you were many years ago. The truth of the matter was stated by Jesus 2,000 years ago, "Then He said, "Assuredly, I say to you, no prophet is accepted in his own country" (Luke 4:24).

When Jesus returned to his hometown after being away for years, he preached His gospel to the home folks. What was their reaction? "So all those in the synagogue, when they heard these things, were filled with wrath, and rose up and thrust Him out of the city; and they led Him to the brow of the hill on which their city was built, that they might throw Him down over the cliff. Then passing through the midst of them, He went His way" (Luke 4:28-30).

Jesus Knows How You Feel When You Lose Loved Ones To Death

If you have never lost a loved one to death, just wait a little longer. It will happen. We all experience the death of a loved one and it is almost impossible to prepare oneself for such an event in life. Even when we know death is imminent, it is hard to accept that we really won't have that loved one around anymore.

Jesus knew what it was like to lose a loved one. He had a friend that he loved very much. This friend was a man named Lazarus. When news reached Jesus that his friend had died, it troubled Him greatly. Jesus left to go to the family of His friend, which included His friends Mary and Martha, sisters of Lazarus. John tells the story: "Then, when Mary came where Jesus was, and saw Him, she fell down at His feet, saying to Him, 'Lord, if You had been here, my brother would not have died.' Therefore, when Jesus saw her weeping, and the Jews who came with her weeping, He groaned in the spirit and was troubled. And He said, 'Where have you laid him?' They said to Him, 'Lord, come and see.' Jesus wept. Then the Jews said, 'See how He loved him'" (John 11:32-36)!

On one occasion, Jesus passed by a city called Nain. He and his disciples noticed a funeral procession coming from the city. A large crowd followed the body of a dead man. The dead man was the only son of a widow, and Jesus, knowing this, was touched by the son's death. The Bible says, "When the Lord saw her, He had compassion on her and said to her, 'Do not weep.' Then He came and touched the open coffin, and those who carried him stood still. And He said, 'Young man, I say to you, arise.' So he who was dead sat up and began to speak. And He presented him to his mother" (Luke 7:13-15).

From this passage, we can see that Jesus knows our suffering when we lose a loved one to death. Jesus knows how we feel and Jesus cares about our feelings. In Luke 4:18, Jesus (quoting from Isaiah 49:8-9) said, "The Spirit of the LORD [is] upon Me, Because He has anointed Me to preach the gospel to [the] poor; **He has sent Me to heal the brokenhearted**, to proclaim liberty to [the] captives and recovery of sight to [the] blind, to set at liberty those who are oppressed."

Jesus Knows How You Feel When You Have Family Problems

Jesus told the parable of the prodigal son who was given his inheritance by his father. The young man, like many today, couldn't wait to leave home and did so immediately upon receiving his inheritance. But when he lost all his wealth, he also lost his friends, and was to the point of starvation. He had to take one of the most humiliating jobs a Jew could have—feeding the unclean pigs.

The young man realized what a mess he had made of his life and determined to go back home and to be a servant to his father. Luke tells the story: "But when he came to himself, he said, 'How many of my father's hired servants have bread enough and to spare, and I perish with hunger! I will arise and go to my father, and will say to him, "Father, I have sinned against heaven and before you, and I am no longer worthy to be called your son. Make me like one of your hired servants." '

"And he arose and came to his father. But when he was still a great way off, his father saw him and had compassion, and ran and fell on his neck and kissed him. And the son said to him, 'Father, I have sinned against heaven and in your sight, and am no longer worthy to be called your son.'

"But the father said to his servants, 'Bring out the best robe and put *it* on him, and put a ring on his hand and sandals on *his* feet. And bring the fatted calf here and kill *it,* and let us eat and be merry; for this my son was dead and is alive again; he was lost and is found.' And they began to be merry" (Luke 15:17-24).

Jesus Knows How You Feel When You Are Burdened With Sins Of The Lost

One of the most devastating things in the life of a Christian is to know that someone you love does not love the Lord and does not desire to do His will. It is a burden that is difficult to bear because you know the consequences of rejecting Christ.

Jesus was so concerned about the salvation of mankind that He died for us. He mourned over the lost on several occasions. He mourned over Jerusalem, knowing the fate that the city would suffer within the next generation—that being total destruction. "Now as He drew near, He saw the city and wept over it, saying, "If you had known, even you, especially in this your day, the things *that make* for your peace! But now they are hidden from your eyes. For days will come upon you when your enemies will build an embankment around you, surround you and close you in on every side, and level you, and your children within you, to the ground; and they will not leave in you one stone upon another, because you did not know the time of your visitation" (Luke 19:41-44). Again Jesus lamented over Jerusalem when he said, "O Jerusalem, Jerusalem, the one who kills the prophets and stones those who are sent to her! How often I wanted to gather your children together, as a hen gathers her chicks under *her* wings, but you were not willing" (Matthew 23:37)!

Jesus also became moved with compassion when He saw the multitudes that were lost. Notice this passage: "But when He saw the multitudes, He was moved with compassion for them, because they were weary and scattered, like sheep having no shepherd. Then He said to His disciples, "The harvest truly *is* plentiful, but the laborers *are* few. Therefore pray the Lord of the harvest to send out laborers into His harvest" (Matthew 9:36-38).

People that have given their lives to God know how painful the burden of sin can be. Such great sorrow is experienced for wrongs and hurts to others and to the cause of Christ. The beauty of the gospel of Christ is that Christ can remove that great burden from us and make us free from sin and guilt.

Jesus yearned for all to come to Him to receive rest for their souls. "Come to Me, all you who labor and are heavy laden, and I will give you rest. Take My yoke upon you and learn from Me, for I am gentle and lowly in heart, and you will find rest for your souls. For My yoke is easy and My burden is light" (Matthew11:28-30).

Keep in mind that Jesus paid the price for our sins, though He was sinless. "Who Himself bore our sins in His own body on the tree, that we, having died to sins, might live for righteousness—by whose stripes you were healed" (1 Peter 2:24). Even though He was sinless, "For He made Him who knew no sin to be sin for us, that we might become the righteousness of God in Him" (2 Corinthians 5:21). The Hebrews writer said, "Who being the brightness of *His* glory and the express image of His person, and upholding all things by the word of His power, when He had by Himself purged our sins, sat down at the right hand of the Majesty on high" (Hebrews 1:3).

Conclusion

Jesus is on our side—defending us, pleading our case or cause. What a great blessing for the children of God, to know that Jesus is our Advocate (1 John 2:1).

You are special to Him. You are so special that Jesus left the joys of heaven to come to earth and experience life as a man with all its disappointments and hardships, and to die for your salvation. He understood persecution, financial problems, rejection, betrayal, criticism, being misunderstood, family problems, and He fully understands the burden of sin, having suffered and died for our sins. His death was in order that His blood could wash away our sins. Revelation 1:5 says, "…To Him who loved us and washed us from our sins in His own blood."

Isn't it nice to know that you are "Special to God."

Chapter 7

You Are Special to God Because His Son Died For You

"For when we were still without strength, in due time Christ died for the ungodly."

Romans 5:6

In Luke Chapter 24, we find an interesting story recorded by Luke, the physician. In this passage, we find Jesus, following the resurrection, walking on the road to Emmaus and talking to two men. These men, not knowing they are talking to Jesus, were discussing the death of Jesus. During the course of the conversation, Jesus said in verse twenty-six, "Ought not the Christ to have suffered these things and to enter into His glory"? And verse twenty-seven says, "And beginning at Moses and all the prophets, he expounded unto them in all the scriptures the things concerning himself." Luke continues the story by saying, "Then He said to them, 'These are the words which I spoke to you while I was still with you, that all things must be fulfilled which were written in the Law of Moses and the Prophets and the Psalms concerning Me.' And He opened their understanding, that they might comprehend the Scriptures. Then He said to them, 'Thus it is written, and thus it was necessary for the Christ to suffer and to rise from the dead the third day, and that repentance and remission of sins should be preached in His name to all nations, beginning at Jerusalem'" (Luke 24: 44-47).

Now, did you grasp what Jesus said? He said His death and resurrection were necessary in order that repentance and remission of sins be preached. Without Christ dying for our sins, there would be no remission of sins. John said, "To Him that loved us and washed us from our sins in His own blood" (Revelation 1:5). The sacrifice of Jesus on the cross was necessary for the salvation of men.

Just as Jesus directed the men from Emmaus to the Old Testament scriptures for proof that Jesus was to die, let's look at some Old Testament prophesies that point out the same thing.

The Old Testament Prophesied About The Death Of Jesus

Remember, Jesus said of the Old Testament scriptures that prophecies of His suffering were "written in the Law of Moses, and the Prophets, and the Psalms concerning Me" (Luke 24:44). Let us look at an example of this prophecy from each of those divisions of the Old Testament.

The Law of Moses prophesied about the coming of Jesus. The first prophecy in the Bible concerning Jesus is found in Genesis 3:15, which says, "And I will put enmity between you and the woman, and between your seed and her Seed; he shall bruise your head, and you shall bruise His heel." This prophecy points out that the Seed of woman, Christ, would be the enemy of Satan, the serpent to whom God was talking. Satan would bruise the heel of Christ, that is, figuratively, to bring about Christ's death. But Christ would arise from the dead and ultimately be victorious not only over death, but over Satan. As God said, "he shall bruise your head." The commentary of Jamieson, Fausset, and Brown, on Genesis 3:15, says, "The serpent wounds the heel that crushes him; and so Satan would be permitted to afflict the humanity of Christ and bring suffering and persecution on His people. The serpent's poison is lodged in its head; and a bruise on that part is fatal. Thus, fatal shall be the stroke which Satan shall receive from Christ, though it is probable he did not at first understand the nature and extent of his doom."

The Psalms speak of the death of Jesus. The greatest of the Messianic Psalms is Psalms 22. In this psalm, we read of the crucifixion of Jesus a thousand years before it took place. Notice a few verses of this psalm: "I am poured out like water, and all My bones are out of joint; my heart is like wax; it has melted within Me. My strength is dried up like a potsherd, and My tongue clings to My jaws; you have brought Me to the dust of death. For dogs have surrounded Me; the congregation of the wicked has enclosed Me. They pierced My hands and My feet; I can count all My bones. They look and stare at Me. They divide My garments among them, and for My clothing they cast lots" (Psalms 22:14-18). As we said, this psalm was written 1,000 years before the crucifixion of Christ. Only by inspiration of God could the psalmist write these things.

The prophets speak of Jesus. About 750 years before Christ, Isaiah, the prophet, spoke of the death of Jesus. Isaiah 53 is one of the great prophecies about Jesus. "Who has believed our report? And to whom has the arm of the

LORD been revealed? For He shall grow up before Him as a tender plant, and as a root out of dry ground. He has no form or comeliness; and when we see Him, there is no beauty that we should desire Him. He is despised and rejected by men, a Man of sorrows and acquainted with grief. And we hid, as it were, our faces from Him; he was despised, and we did not esteem Him. Surely **He has borne our griefs and carried our sorrows;** yet **we esteemed Him stricken, smitten by God, and afflicted.** But He was **wounded for our transgressions, he was bruised for our iniquities;** the chastisement for our peace was upon Him, and **by His stripes we are healed.** All we like sheep have gone astray; we have turned, every one, to his own way; and the LORD has laid on Him the iniquity of us all. He was oppressed and He was afflicted, yet He opened not His mouth; **he was led as a lamb to the slaughter, and as a sheep before its shearers is silent,** so He opened not His mouth. He was taken from prison and from judgment, and who will declare His generation? For **He was cut off from the land of the living; for the transgressions of My people He was stricken.** And they made His grave with the wicked—but with the rich at His death, because He had done no violence, nor was any deceit in His mouth. Yet **it pleased the LORD to bruise Him;** he has put Him to grief. When You make His soul an offering for sin, he shall see His seed, He shall prolong His days, and the pleasure of the LORD shall prosper in His hand. He shall see the labor of His soul, and be satisfied. By His knowledge My righteous Servant shall justify many, for He shall bear their iniquities. Therefore I will divide Him a portion with the great, and He shall divide the spoil with the strong, because He poured out His soul unto death, and He was numbered with the transgressors, and **He bore the sin of many, and made intercession for the transgressors"** (Isaiah 53:1-12).

Was The Death Of Jesus Planned, Or Was It An Accident?

Many people today have been taught that Jesus came to the earth to establish an earthly kingdom, but failed in doing so. All hopes of this plan ended when He was crucified. They teach that since Jesus failed in His mission of establishing a world kingdom, God substituted the "church age" in which we live today. And someday Jesus will return to the earth to establish His kingdom for a thousand years on earth.

I find some problems with this theology. First, if Christ failed to establish a kingdom the first time, what is the guarantee that He will succeed the next time? Can anyone honestly believe that Christ failed in His mission? Can the creature keep the Creator from His mission? When Christ died, and the church was established, was this the result of a failed mission on the part of God? Absolutely not! This was God's plan from before the beginning of time.

We have already looked at Luke 24, where Jesus pointed out that He was supposed to die. We looked at Moses (Genesis 3:15), David (Psalm 22), and Isaiah (Isaiah 53). All of these Old Testament prophets told us the same thing— Christ must die!

Now, let's turn to the New Testament and see what is revealed on this matter. When Peter preached the first gospel sermon in Acts 2, we find that he spoke about the plan of God. He said, "Him, being **delivered by the determined purpose and foreknowledge of God,** you have taken by lawless hands, have crucified, and put to death" (Acts 2:23). We see from this passage that it was God's plan for Jesus to die for us, and in doing so, fulfilled Old Testament prophesies. In Acts 3:18, Luke writes, "But those things which **God foretold by the mouth of all His prophets, that the Christ would suffer,** He has thus fulfilled." And in Acts

4:27-28, he writes, "For truly against Your holy Servant Jesus, whom You anointed, both Herod and Pontius Pilate, with the Gentiles and the people of Israel, **were gathered together to do whatever Your hand and Your purpose determined before to be done."** Later on in the Book of Acts, when Paul was preaching at Thessalonica, we find Paul was **"explaining and demonstrating that the Christ had to suffer and rise again from the dead,** and *saying,* 'This Jesus whom I preach to you is the Christ'" (Acts 17:2-4).

From these passages, how could one believe that Jesus had His plan foiled by earthly powers and that God could not carry out His plan of Jesus dying on the cross for the remission of our sins?

The Precious Blood Of Christ

The shedding of the blood of Jesus on the cross made it possible for us to have the remission of our sins. God, who had demanded a blood sacrifice from the time of Cain and Abel, required the blood of His Son for the forgiveness of our sins. This should help us realize the enormity and the severity of sin, and how precious the blood of Christ should be to us. In fact, Jesus, on the night He was betrayed, "took the cup, and gave thanks, and gave it to them, saying, 'Drink from it, all of you. For **this is My blood of the new covenant, which is shed for many for the remission of sins'"** (Matthew 26:27-28).

Peter tells us we "were not redeemed with corruptible things, like silver or gold, from your aimless conduct received by tradition from your fathers, but with the precious blood of Christ, as of a lamb without blemish and without spot" (1 Peter 1:18-19).

John tells us that "if we walk in the light as He is in the light, we have fellowship with one another, and the blood of Jesus Christ His Son cleanses us from all sin. If we say that

86

we have no sin, we deceive ourselves, and the truth is not in us. If we confess our sins, He is faithful and just to forgive us our sins and to cleanse us from all unrighteousness. If we say that we have not sinned, we make Him a liar, and His word is not in us" (1 John1:7-10).

The apostle Paul tells us that "In Him we have redemption through His blood, the forgiveness of sins, according to the riches of His grace" (Ephesians 1:7). Paul also says in the Colossian letter that it is Jesus "in whom we have redemption through His blood, the forgiveness of sins" (Colossians 1:14). In the Roman letter, Paul says, "Much more then, having now been justified by His blood, we shall be saved from wrath through Him" (Romans 5:9).

Not only was the blood of Christ shed for the remission of our sins, it was shed to pay the price of the Lord's church. "Therefore take heed to yourselves and to all the flock, among which the Holy Spirit has made you overseers, to shepherd the church of God **which He purchased with His own blood"** (Acts 20:28). Christ purchased the church with "His own blood." The church is Christ's church, and He has all authority over it (Matthew 28:18). Therefore, we should strive to worship Christ as He has shown us in the New Testament, and remember that our worship is to be directed toward God, and not to please ourselves.

The Death of Jesus Is In Vain If We Do Not Have Faith In Him

Yes, Jesus died so that we might have remission of our sins. But, what about man's part in salvation? Man's part of the salvation equation is faith. Biblical faith involves more than belief; it involves a conviction of mind, a trust of heart, and a surrender of will. Based on scriptural evidence, our minds are convicted of the story of Christ and the need to be obedient to Him. Based on what we read in scripture, we grow to the point of trusting that God will keep His end of the bargain (salvation), if we keep our end of the bargain (faithfulness). Then, we surrender our will. God's will now becomes more important to us than our own will—it is now God who directs our lives and our decisions. In fact, it is impossible to please God without faith. "But without faith it is impossible to please Him, for he who comes to God must believe that He is, and that He is a rewarder of those who diligently seek Him" (Hebrews 11:6).

Indeed, it is through God's grace and by our faith that we are saved. "For by grace you have been saved through faith, and that not of yourselves; it is the gift of God" (Ephesians 2:8). However, we must remember that this salvation would not be possible without the shedding of the blood of Jesus on the cross.

It is by faith that we are right or just in God's sight. Paul said, "Therefore, having been justified by faith, we have peace with God through our Lord Jesus Christ, through whom also we have access by faith into this grace in which we stand, and rejoice in hope of the glory of God" (Romans 5:1-2). Because of this faith, we have access to God. Paul says, "In whom we have boldness and access with confidence through faith in Him" (Ephesians 3:12).

Christ Died For You

As we explore the thought that we are special to God, we must remember that we are so special that our salvation required the blood of a Savior—Jesus Christ. The Bible says that Christ dwells in our hearts through faith (Ephesians 3:17), and that faith is our assurance of the thing we hope for, yet cannot see. That is a home in heaven for the saved. (Hebrews 11:1).

The Bible teaches emphatically that we must obey our Lord in order to have this salvation. Just as Jesus was obedient to the Father, we are to be obedient to Christ. The Hebrews writer said, "Though He was a Son, yet He learned obedience by the things which He suffered. And having been perfected, He became the author of eternal salvation to all who obey Him" (Hebrews 5:8-9).

There is a serious warning in the Bible to those who do not recognize the authority of Jesus Christ and do not honor Him as God's Son. "Of how much worse punishment, do you suppose, will he be thought worthy who has trampled the Son of God underfoot, counted the blood of the covenant by which he was sanctified a common thing, and insulted the Spirit of grace? For we know Him who said, 'Vengeance is Mine; I will repay,' says the Lord. And again, 'The Lord will judge His people.' It is a fearful thing to fall into the hands of the living God" (Hebrews 10:29-31).

The death of Jesus on the cross demonstrates God's great love for us. Certainly, this is "the greatest story ever told." By His "amazing grace," the Son of God left the joys of heaven and came to earth in order to die for us. We must be very "Special to God."

Chapter 8

You Are Special to God Because His Church Was Built For You

"And I also say to you that you are Peter, and on this rock I will build My church, and the gates of Hades shall not prevail against it."

Matthew 16:18

The church that God built for you is a very special institution. The church came into existence in the mind of God before the world was ever created. It was designed according to God's plan and paid for by the blood of Christ on the cross. Acts 20:28 tells us, "Therefore take heed to yourselves and to all the flock, among which the Holy Spirit has made you overseers, to shepherd the church of God which He purchased with His own blood." The church was a mystery of God that was revealed in the New Testament, and this church was built for you. It cost the blood of Christ which He freely shed for you. If the Father and the Son would do this for you, then surely you must indeed be "Special to God."

Scripture reveals to us that the plan for the church had been a mystery, hidden by God, until the time it was revealed. Notice this passage: "And to make all see what *is* the fellowship of the mystery, which from the beginning of the ages has been hidden in God Who created all things through Jesus Christ; to the intent that now the manifold wisdom of God might be made known by the church to the principalities and powers in the heavenly *places,* according to the eternal purpose which He accomplished in Christ Jesus our Lord" (Ephesians 3:9-11). The church was a part of God's eternal purpose and plan for His people. How special we are that we can be members of that church.

Some teach that Jesus came to the earth to establish an earthly kingdom and failed in His mission. This is so-o-o-o wrong! Jesus came to establish a spiritual kingdom—His church. And you can be the recipient of this great gift of God to man.

When Jesus was arrested and brought before Pilate and Pilate questioned Jesus, Jesus said, "My kingdom is not of this world. If My kingdom were of this world, My servants would fight, so that I should not be delivered to the Jews; but now My kingdom is not from here" (John 18:36).

The Church Is Prophesied

There are many Old Testament prophecies of the church. However, we will only look at two found in the New Testament. In Matthew, chapter eighteen, Jesus said, "And I also say to you that you are Peter, and on this rock I will build My church, and the gates of Hades shall not prevail against it. And I will give you the keys of the kingdom of heaven, and whatever you bind on earth will be bound in heaven, and whatever you loose on earth will be loosed in heaven" (Matthew 16:18-20).

The "rock" Jesus refers to in this passage is the confession that Peter made about who Christ was. In verse 16, Peter said, "You are the Christ, the Son of the living God." Jesus is the one on whom the church is built.

Another prophecy of the establishment of the church is found in Mark 9:1. In this passage, Jesus said, "Assuredly, I say to you that there are some standing here who will not taste death till they see the kingdom of God present with power." If the church (the kingdom of God) was not established during the lifetime of some of the people to which Jesus was talking, then there are some 2,000 year old folks around today, because Jesus said that some of them would be alive when the kingdom was established.

The Church Comes Into Existence

We can read in the Bible of the Lord's church coming into existence. This is recorded for us in Acts chapter 2, following Christ's ascension back to heaven. Luke, the writer of Acts, records for us this account. The establishment of the church was preceded by the Holy Spirit coming upon the twelve apostles and allowing them to have the miraculous gift of speaking in tongues. This meant that when the apostles spoke, everyone present could understand the apostles' speech in their own language.

The occasion of this great event was the day of Pentecost, occurring fifty days after the Passover. This fiftieth day following the Passover would be on a Sunday. The New Testament church was established on a Sunday and it met on Sundays (1Corinthians 16:1-2; Acts 20:7). The date of the establishment of the church is around 33 AD.

On this particular day in Jerusalem, there were Jews gathered from many countries to celebrate Pentecost. The

Lord chose this day for the announcement of His gospel (His power to save man) and the establishment of His church. On this day, Peter and the other apostles spoke of the salvation of the Lord. Peter, the principal speaker, accused the Jews of crucifying Jesus. He said, "You have taken by lawless hands, have crucified, and put to death" (Acts 2:23). Again in verse 36, Peter said, "Therefore let all the house of Israel know assuredly that God has made this Jesus, whom you crucified, both Lord and Christ."

The Jews, realizing that they were guilty of crucifying Jesus, were remorseful and cried out to Peter asking what they must do in order to be saved (Acts 2:37). Peter's response was, "Repent, and let every one of you be baptized in the name of Jesus Christ for the remission of sins; and you shall receive the gift of the Holy Spirit" (Acts 2:38).

The Bible goes on to tell us that those who accepted Christ that day were baptized for the remission of sins, and these saved individuals were added to the Lord's church. Luke says, they were "praising God and having favor with all the people. And the Lord added to the church daily those who were being saved" (Acts 2:47).

It is interesting to note that all the scriptures concerning the church, prior to Acts 2, point to the coming of the church, and all scriptures after Acts 2, concerning the church, point out that the church now existed. Of the 110 times the church is mentioned in the New Testament, it is only mentioned three times before Acts 2 in the future tense, and after Acts 2, it is mentioned in the past tense 107 times.

Jesus Is The Founder Of The Church

The church that Jesus died for was founded by Jesus Himself. It is His church and should wear His name. Notice some characteristics of Jesus' church.

Jesus is the purchaser of the church. As we pointed out earlier, Jesus bought the church with His own blood. He died so the church could come into existence and so the saved could be members of that church. In Acts 20:28, Luke, speaking to the elders of the church at Ephesus, records for us that "...the Holy Spirit has made you overseers, to shepherd the church of God which He purchased with His own blood."

Jesus is the head of the church. Not only did Jesus pay for the church, He is the head of the church. Paul writes, "For the husband is head of the wife, as also Christ is head of the church; and He is the Savior of the body" (Ephesians 5:23).

Jesus is the Savior of the church. Notice the previous passage teaches that Christ "...is the Savior of the body" (Ephesians 5:23). The body is the church, according to Ephesians 1:22-23. This says, "And He put all *things* under His feet, and gave Him *to be* head over all *things* to the church, which is His body, the fullness of Him who fills all in all."

Jesus is the builder of the church. Remember the conversation Jesus had with Peter in Matthew 16 where Jesus said, "And I also say to you that you are Peter, and on this rock I will build My church, and the gates of Hades shall not prevail against it" (Matthew 16:18). Jesus promised to build His church, and He did. Jesus is the rock on which the church is built. He built this church for you.

Jesus is the foundation of the church. Again, Matthew 16 teaches that Jesus would build His church upon the foundation that He was "the Son of the Living God" (Matthew 16:16). Paul wrote in 1 Corinthians 3:10 that in his work for the church, he laid the foundation for others to build upon. Paul went about starting new churches and others built on that work. But Paul said that Jesus was the foundation of the church. "For no other foundation can anyone lay than that which is laid, which is Jesus Christ" (1 Corinthians 3:11).

Jesus is the chief cornerstone of the church. In the analogy of a physical building, the spiritual institution of the church is mentioned as having a cornerstone. In times past, a cornerstone was the most perfect stone which was laid first and the rest of the structure was laid out according to this squared cornerstone. The analogy is used in the church. Jesus is the "chief cornerstone" of the church. It was laid out on Him—that is, He gave it the proper shape. Notice 1 Peter 2:6-8, "Therefore it is also contained in the Scripture, "Behold, I lay in Zion a chief cornerstone, elect, precious, and he who believes on Him will by no means be put to shame. Therefore, to you who believe, He is precious; but to those who are disobedient, 'The stone which the builders rejected has become the chief cornerstone,' and 'A stone of stumbling and a rock of offense.' They stumble, being disobedient to the word, to which they also were appointed."

The Worship Of The New Testament Church

Jesus, speaking to the Samaritan woman at the well, told her, "God is Spirit, and those who worship Him must worship in spirit and truth" (John 4:24). "In spirit" means with the proper frame of mind, meditating on spiritual things rather than things of this world when we worship God. "In truth" means that we are to worship according to the pattern that God gave man for worship. This is clearly seen in a study of the scriptures concerning the New Testament church.

Communion was a part of the worship of the New Testament church. The expression, "breaking of bread," is used in the Bible as a reference to partaking of the Communion, or the Lord's Supper. We are told in Acts 2:42 that the new converts in Jerusalem did this. "And they continued steadfastly in the apostles' doctrine and fellowship, in the breaking of bread, and in prayers." Acts 20:7 tells us, "Now on the first *day* of the week, when the disciples came together to break bread, Paul, ready to depart the next day, spoke to them and continued his message until midnight."

Singing was a part of worship of the New Testament Church. There are many scriptures that show that singing was a part of New Testament worship, but space will not allow a complete study of the subject. But briefly, Paul tells us that Christians were to speak "to one another in psalms and hymns and spiritual songs, singing and making melody in your heart to the Lord" (Ephesians 5:19). In Colossians 3:16, Paul said, "Let the word of Christ dwell in you richly in all wisdom, teaching and admonishing one another in psalms and hymns and spiritual songs, singing with grace in your hearts to the Lord."

Praying was a part of worship in the New Testament Church. Several churches in the New Testament are recorded as praying churches. Among these are the churches at Jerusalem, Philippi, Corinth, Colosse, Thessalonica, and Tyre. Acts 12:5 tells us that when Peter was arrested, "**constant prayer was offered to God for him by the church.**" Churches also prayed for particular things, as in selecting elders to lead the church. Luke records for us, "So when they had appointed elders in every church, and prayed with fasting, they commended them to the Lord in whom they had believed" (Acts 14:23). Acts 2:42 tells us that the church continued steadfastly "in prayers."

Giving was a part of the worship of the New Testament church. Paul says, speaking of the collection, "So let each one give as he purposes in his heart, not grudgingly or of necessity; for God loves a cheerful giver" (2 Corinthians 9:7).

Teaching and preaching were a part of the worship of the New Testament church. The apostle Paul told the church in Rome, "I am ready to preach the gospel to you..." (Romans 1:15). What better place to preach to Christians than in the assembly of the church. But perhaps the best passage to show that preaching was a part of the worship of the New Testament church is found in Acts 20:7, a verse we often use to point out the importance of partaking of the Lord's Supper in worship. In this passage, we find that Paul spoke in the assembly of the church. We are told, "...Paul, ready to depart the next day, spoke to them and continued his message until midnight" (Acts 20:7).

Conclusion

Space will not allow the inclusion of the work of the New Testament church. Briefly, the work of the New Testament church is to preach the gospel (1 Corinthians 1:21), edify its members (Ephesians 4:12), and to provide benevolence to needy Christians (Romans 15:25-26).

The plan for the church was implemented by Jesus Christ, the Son of God, who built His church for us, paying the price for the church with His blood. How indebted we should be to God for the glorious blood bought church of Jesus Christ. He did all of this because we are "Special to God."

Chapter 9

You Are Special to God Because His Word Is Spread By You

"The fruit of the righteous is a tree of life, and he who wins souls is wise."

Proverbs 11:30

How thankful we should be that Jesus died for us so that we might live for Him. Living for Jesus involves telling others about our Savior and how He died for us on the cruel cross of Calvary, shedding His precious blood to wash away our sins. Indeed, John wrote in the Book of Revelation, "and from Jesus Christ, the faithful witness, the firstborn from the dead, and the ruler over the kings of the earth. To Him who loved us and washed us from our sins in His own blood" (Revelation 1:5). Jesus paid the price for our salvation, providing for us hope of heaven and a plan for saving man. The clear message of the gospel is salvation through Jesus Christ. Jesus said in Luke 19:10, "For the Son of man is come to seek and save that which is lost." Today, Jesus uses us to do the "seeking", so He can do the "saving". Proverbs 11:30 says, "He that wins souls is wise."

New Testament Examples Of Spreading The Word

In the beginning of Christ's ministry, the twelve apostles spread the word. Beginning with the "Limited Commission," the disciples of Jesus went forth with His message of salvation. The Bible says, "These twelve Jesus sent out and commanded them, saying: 'Do not go into the way of the Gentiles, and do not enter a city of the Samaritans. But go rather to the lost sheep of the house of Israel. And as you go, preach, saying, the kingdom of heaven is at hand. Heal the sick, cleanse the lepers, raise the dead, cast out demons. Freely you have received, freely give. Provide neither gold nor silver nor copper in your money belts, nor bag for your journey, nor two tunics, nor sandals, nor staffs; for a worker is worthy of his food. Now whatever city or town you enter, inquire who in it is worthy, and stay there till you go out. And when you go into a household, greet it. If the household is worthy, let your peace come upon it. But if it is not worthy, let your peace return to you. And whoever will not receive you nor hear your words, when you depart from that house or city, shake off the dust from your feet. Assuredly, I say to you, it will be more tolerable for the land of Sodom and Gomorrah in the Day of Judgment than for that city'" (Matthew 10:5-15)!

Shortly before Christ ascended into heaven, He gave His apostles "The Great Commission." This commission of Christ required that men teach others the truth of the gospel. Notice what Jesus said about spreading the gospel (the good news of Jesus Christ). "Go therefore and make disciples of all the nations, baptizing them in the name of the Father and of the Son and of the Holy Spirit, teaching them to observe all things that I have commanded you; and lo, I am with you always, even to the end of the age. Amen" (Matthew 28:19-20). In the Gospel of Mark, we see Mark's account of the Great Commission. "And He said to them, 'Go into all the world and preach the gospel to every creature. He who believes and is baptized will be saved; but he who does not believe will be condemned" (Mark 16:15-16).

The Great Commission In Action

The Book of Acts has been described as "The Great Commission in action." The book begins with the message from Christ to the disciples that they shall "be witnesses to Me in Jerusalem, and in all Judea and Samaria, and to the end of the earth" (Acts 1:8). In the second chapter of Acts, we have the glorious beginning of the Lord's church on the Day of Pentecost, following the resurrection of Jesus Christ. This beginning was accompanied by various signs and wonders. One of the most significant of these was that the apostles were able to speak in tongues, that is, they were able to speak to the people that had come to Jerusalem from the various nations of the earth and they were able to understand them in their own language. Notice the words of Luke: "And they were all filled with the Holy Spirit and began to speak with other tongues, as the Spirit gave them utterance" (Acts 2:4).

Preaching The Gospel Results In
Church Growth

In Acts 2, when the people realized their need for the gospel of Jesus Christ, they cried out, "men and brethren, what shall we do" (Acts 2:37)? The response of Peter was "Repent, and let every one of you be baptized in the name of Jesus Christ for the remission of sins; and you shall receive the gift of the Holy Spirit" (Acts 2:38). The response to this first gospel invitation was that 3,000 were baptized into Christ for remission of sins (Acts 2:41) and that the people were "praising God and having favor with all the people. And the Lord added to the church daily those who were being saved" (Acts 2:47). In Acts 5:14, we read, "And believers were increasingly added to the Lord, multitudes of both men and women" and in Acts 6:1, "the number of the disciples was multiplying." In Acts 6:7, we find "the number of the disciples multiplied greatly in Jerusalem, and a great many of the priests were obedient to the faith." Acts 9:31 tells us that the churches throughout all Judea, Galilee, and Samaria had peace and were edified, and they were multiplied. Acts 12:24 also tells us that "the word of God grew and multiplied." These biblical examples let us know of the power of God's word and that it can be spread by mankind.

God Uses Man to Spread His Word

One thing that we should notice about the spreading of the gospel is that it was always done by man. God entrusted the gospel into "earthen vessels." This means that God does not operate directly on the hearts of men to convert them, but that His word is spread by men and these efforts result in the conversion of others. We see this in Acts 9:15, where the Lord said for Ananias to go to Paul and teach him what he must do to be a Christian. The Lord said, "Go, for he is a chosen vessel of Mine to bear My name before Gentiles, kings, and the children of Israel." In 2 Corinthians 4:7, Paul said of the gospel, "We have this treasure in earthen vessels that the excellence of the power may be of God and not of us."

Now did you notice these verses carefully? Therein lies a great lesson for each of us, that God uses man to spread His word. Certainly, we must be "Special to God" if He chooses us to spread His word!

Persecuted Christians Spread the Gospel

As much as we hate the thought of religious persecution, we have an example from the Bible where religious persecution resulted in the spread of the gospel. In Acts 7, we see that Stephen was the first Christian martyr. He gave his life for Christ. Refusing to back down from the Jews and pointing out their sins, the Jews stoned Stephen to death. One of those standing nearby and holding the clothes of those who stoned Stephen was a young man named Saul, of Tarsus. This is the Saul that became the apostle Paul and was converted in Damascus under the teaching of Ananias (Acts 9:17-19). Later, Paul would state that Ananias came to tell him what he must do to be saved. He said to Saul, "And now why are you waiting? Arise and be baptized, and wash away your sins, calling on the name of the Lord" (Acts 22:16). This same message is to be preached today and will bring about the same result—the salvation of souls.

Philip Spreads the Gospel in Samaria

"Then Philip went down to the city of Samaria and preached Christ to them. And the multitudes with one accord heeded the things spoken by Philip, hearing and seeing the miracles which he did. For unclean spirits, crying with a loud voice, came out of many who were possessed; and many who were paralyzed and lame were healed. And there was great joy in that city" (Acts 8:5-8). As the gospel begins to spread from Jerusalem and Judea, it goes to Samaria and will then go to "the end of the earth" as Christ declared in Acts 1:8. Indeed, the Book of Acts is a book of conversions.

The Gospel Is Preached to the Gentiles

In Acts chapter 10, we see that Peter preached the gospel to the Gentiles—the household of Cornelius being the first Gentile converts. As the gospel spread among the Gentiles, Paul was enlisted by the church at Antioch to come and work with them and was then sponsored on several missionary journeys to the Gentiles, to spread the gospel of Christ. The success of these first century Christians was so great that Paul proclaimed, "the gospel which you heard, which was preached to every creature under heaven, of which I, Paul, became a minister" (Colossians 1:23). Did you see that? The gospel, during the first century, was carried to the whole world! Who carried it? Individual Christians assumed their responsibility to teach and carried out the "Great Commission" of Jesus Christ.

Why Should I Spread The Word?

Does Jesus expect me to spread His word? The Bible teaches that each individual has a responsibility in this area. Let us look at some reasons why we should teach others the gospel of Christ.

We teach to bear fruit for the master. In the analogy that Jesus makes in John 15:1-6 of Him being the "true vine" and His Father the "vinedresser," Jesus points out that we are "branches" in Him and that we have the responsibility to bear fruit for Him. He says, "I am the vine, you are the branches. He who abides in Me, and I in him, bears much fruit; for without Me you can do nothing. If anyone does not abide in Me, he is cast out as a branch and is withered; and they gather them and throw them into the fire, and they are burned" (John 15:5-6).

We teach to save the souls of others. Bearing fruit in the previous point is the equivalent of saving souls. The Proverbs writer tells us, "The fruit of the righteous is a tree of life, and he who wins souls is wise" (Proverbs 11:30). Are we wise? Are we trying to save souls? Since God has left the responsibility of sharing the gospel in our hands, the job won't get done unless we do it!

We teach others that they might teach. When we learn the gospel, we have a responsibility to pass it on to others. This is what the apostle Paul said to a young gospel preacher by the name of Timothy. He said, "You therefore, my son, be strong in the grace that is in Christ Jesus. And the things that you have heard from me among many witnesses, commit these to faithful men who will be able to teach others also. You therefore must endure hardship as a good soldier of Jesus Christ" (2 Timothy 2:1-3).

To teach requires spiritual growth. In order to share the gospel with others, we have to know what the Bible says. We can only know this by spending the necessary time to read and study our Bibles, learning its truths, and having a willingness to share what we have learned. The King James Version of the Bible renders 2 Timothy 2:15, as "Study to shew thyself approved unto God, a workman that needeth not to be ashamed, rightly dividing the word of truth." Study is required to know God's word. In our busy lives today, too often we fail to study our Bibles as we ought. Let us determine to study our Bibles each day and be ready to share its message with others.

To teach others requires a personal conviction. God saved us so we can save others for Him. After we teach others, we fulfill that obligation to them. They must then save themselves and then grow spiritually to the point that they can go forth and teach others the gospel of Christ. The Hebrews writer warned that some had failed in this—that they should be to the point in their spiritual development that they could teach others, but were not able. The writer of Hebrews says, "For though by this time you ought to be teachers, you need someone to teach you again the first principles of the oracles of God; and you have come to need milk and not solid food. For everyone who partakes only of milk is unskilled in the word of righteousness, for he is a babe. But solid food belongs to those who are of full age, that is, those who by reason of use have their senses exercised to discern both good and evil" (Hebrews 5:12-14).

We teach to prove our discipleship. True discipleship requires self denial. We live in a time in which people don't want to deny themselves of anything. The desire of the day is to heap upon ourselves various pleasures and material possessions, thinking these will bring true happiness. This is how shallow we have become in our thinking. Notice the words of our Savior in this matter: "Then Jesus said to His disciples, 'If anyone desires to come after Me, let him deny himself, and take up his cross, and follow Me. For whoever desires to save his life will lose it, but whoever loses his life for My sake will find it. For what profit is it to a man if he gains the whole world, and loses his own soul? Or what will a man give in exchange for his soul? For the Son of Man will come in the glory of His Father with His angels, and then He will reward each according to his works'" (Matthew 16:24-27).

What Can I Do To Spread The Gospel?

Most of us have our inadequacies and feel that we do not have the power or ability to bring someone to Christ. However, the power is from God and the ability is what God has given us to carry out His will. The problem is that many of us say, "I can't," and we don't try to share what we have learned about Christ, His Church, and our own salvation. Let's look at some things we can do to spread the gospel.

We can pray. Since the time Jesus walked on the earth, there has been a greater harvest than there are laborers to bring in the harvest. As Jesus uses the story of laborers and harvest, he is not talking about crops, but souls that need to be "harvested" for Christ. Notice this passage: "But when He saw the multitudes, He was moved with compassion for them, because they were weary and scattered, like sheep having no shepherd. Then He said to His disciples, 'The harvest truly is plentiful, but the laborers are few. Therefore pray the Lord of the harvest to send out laborers into His harvest'" (Matthew 9:36-38).

We can prepare ourselves to teach. In order to be successful in any work, we must learn about the trade and become proficient in it. The same is true with teaching the gospel. We must train ourselves or have others train us in order that we might be prepared for this work. As we stated earlier, Paul told Timothy that he should "commit these to faithful men who will be able to teach others also" (2 Timothy 2:2).

We can have a zeal for lost souls. When we fully realize that those who do not know the gospel will be lost, we should have a greater zeal to share the gospel with them. Paul said that when the Lord returns, He will come "in flaming fire taking vengeance on those who do not know God, and on those who do not obey the gospel of our Lord Jesus Christ. These shall be punished with everlasting destruction from the presence of the Lord and from the glory of His power" (2 Thessalonians 1:8-9).

We can take advantage of opportunities. There are many ways you can share your faith. Invite friends to worship services, give out tracts, tapes, CD's, and periodicals. Invite people into your home. Ask if they would study with you. When asked a religious question, give an honest answer. If you don't know the answer, find it in the Bible, God's Holy Word.

Don't make excuses not to study. Don't be too busy for Bible study. Don't say you don't know enough. Don't worry about being embarrassed. Don't be ashamed of the gospel. Paul said, "For I am not ashamed of the gospel of Christ, for it is the power of God to salvation for everyone who believes, for the Jew first and also for the Greek" (Romans 1:16-17). Peter said, "Be ready to give a defense to everyone who asks you a reason for the hope that is in you, with meekness and fear" (1 Peter 3:15).

Conclusion

Just as in the New Testament times, God uses us today to spread His word. We must be very special to God because of the special task He has given us. If we could not do this work, God would not have given it to us.

Let each of us take a closer look at the responsibility placed on us to teach the word of God as we have opportunity. As we do this work, let us be reminded that God has given us this work because we are "Special to God!"

Chapter 10

You Are Special to God Because His Son Is Your Shepherd

"Know that the LORD, He *is* God; It is He *who* has made us, and not we ourselves; we are His people and the sheep of His pasture."

Psalm 100:3

Psalm 23—"A Psalm of David. The LORD *is* my shepherd; I shall not want. He makes me to lie down in green pastures; He leads me beside the still waters. He restores my soul; He leads me in the paths of righteousness for His name's sake. Yea, though I walk through the valley of the shadow of death, I will fear no evil; For You *are* with me; Your rod and Your staff, they comfort me. You prepare a table before me in the presence of my enemies; You anoint my head with oil; My cup runs over. Surely goodness and mercy shall follow me all the days of my life; and I will dwell in the house of the LORD Forever."

There is no passage in the word of God that is loved more and provides more comfort than the 23rd Psalm. It has been the source of comfort to Christians when the chips are down and hearts are heavy because of trials that they face in their journey of life. Perhaps the 23rd Psalm is the best loved passage of the entire Bible. Charles Swindoll, in his book, Living Beyond the Daily Grind, Book 1, mentions some times in people's lives when they turn to the 23rd Psalm.

- Parents whose children have decided to leave the Lord for sin and degradation.
- The soldier in battle, fearing injury and possible death.
- The grieving widow standing over a fresh grave wondering how her life will go on.
- The guilty wanderer seeking forgiveness and direction.
- The lonely stranger longing for love and companionship.
- The orphaned and the forgotten.
- Suffering saint strapped to the bed of pain.
- The depressed and the jobless.
- The prison inmate and the persecuted.
- The prodigal and the divorced.

Why has this passage—this psalm, become so loved by so many? I think the answer is that it causes one to focus on our relationship with God and His loving kindness, care, and protection of His people. Remember that we are "Special to God" because of our relationship with Him.

Let us analyze the psalm of a shepherd. David was a "man after God's own heart" (Acts 13:22). He was the "sweet psalmist of Israel" (2 Samuel 23:1). The author of this psalm was a shepherd who thoroughly understood the relationship of the shepherd to his sheep, and it was this shepherd that noted the analogy of God serving as a shepherd to His people. David notes that it is God who cares for us, feeds us, provides for us, protects us, comforts us, goes with us through the darkest days of our lives, and ultimately leads us through death to eternal life with Him! What comfort! What joy to have such a Shepherd!

Please notice these two additional psalms that show that the Lord is our Shepherd.

Psalm 79:13 So we, Your people and sheep of Your pasture, Will give You thanks forever; We will show forth Your praise to all generations.

Psalm 100:3 Know that the LORD, He *is* God; It is He *who* has made us, and not we ourselves; we are His people and the sheep of His pasture.

When we fully understand the importance of being the sheep in the Lord's pasture, then we can understand our importance in the sight of God.

"The Lord Is My Shepherd"
(That's personal)

To better understand the relationship of sheep to the shepherd, we need to understand the role of the shepherd.

The role of a shepherd. The role of the shepherd is to care for the sheep. In this simple sentence, we find capsulated the far reaching and detailed work of raising sheep and the producing of wool. Let's take time to read what Jesus said about being a shepherd.

"'Most assuredly, I say to you, I am the door of the sheep. All who *ever* came before Me are thieves and robbers, but the sheep did not hear them. I am the door. If anyone enters by Me, he will be saved, and will go in and out and find pasture. The thief does not come except to steal, and to kill, and to destroy. I have come that they may have life, and that they may have *it* more abundantly. I am the good shepherd. The good shepherd gives His life for the sheep. But a hireling, *he who is* not the shepherd, one who does not own the sheep, sees the wolf coming and leaves the sheep and flees; and the wolf catches the sheep and scatters them. The hireling flees because he is a hireling and does not care about the sheep. I am the good shepherd; and I know My *sheep,* and am known by My own. As the Father knows Me, even so I know the Father; and I lay down My life for the sheep. And other sheep I have which are not of this fold; them also I must bring, and they will hear My voice; and there will be one flock *and* one shepherd. 'Therefore My Father loves Me, because I lay down My life that I may take it again. No one takes it from Me, but I lay it down of Myself. I have power to lay it down, and I have power to take it again. This command I have received from My Father'" (John 10:7-18).

The Lord is my personal Shepherd! A shepherd takes on a number of responsibilities when caring for sheep. As my Shepherd, Jesus took on the following responsibilities:

1. The Lord is concerned about me.
2. He leads me.
3. He feeds me.
4. He nurtures me.
5. He shelters me.
6. He comforts me.
7. He keeps me safe.
8. He seeks me when I am lost.

9. He brings me back to the fold.
10. He fights for me. This is seen in the life of King David. As a shepherd boy, he said to Saul, "Your servant used to keep his father's sheep, and when a lion or a bear came and took a lamb out of the flock, I went out after it and struck it, and delivered the lamb from its mouth; and when it arose against me, I caught it by its beard, and struck and killed it" (1 Samuel 17:34-35).
11. He is with me in my darkest days.
12. He died for me.
13. He lives for me.
14. He is my door to eternal life!

Because the Lord is my Shepherd, I shall not want. Sheep are free from wants when their needs are met—food, water, shorn of their wool, free from disease, parasites, and are sheltered. These are all physical needs of the sheep. David is speaking of spiritual needs for the child of God. The child of God—the sheep of His pasture, do not want for anything when their spiritual needs are met.

As the shepherd makes the sheep content, we are to find contentment. The Greek word translated content means: to be enough, suffice, be sufficient. One of the great problems we face today is that of contentment. Yet God says we are to be content. Paul said, "Not that I speak in regard to need, for I have learned in whatever state I am, to be content" (Philippians 4:11). Later, he said, "Now godliness with contentment is great gain" (1 Timothy 6:6), "and having food and clothing, with these we shall be content" (1 Timothy 6:8). The Hebrews writer said, "Let your conduct *be* without covetousness; *be* content with such things as you have. For He Himself has said, 'I will never leave you nor forsake you'" (Hebrews 13:5).

Have you found contentment in life? Are you happy with yourself? Do you see yourself as one who never is satisfied—as one who never has enough? Our Lord says we need to find contentment.

"He Makes Me Lie Down In Green Pastures"

"Green pastures did not just happen by chance. Green pastures were the product of tremendous labor, time, and skill in land use. Green pastures were the result of clearing rough, rocky land; of tearing out brush and roots and stumps; of deep plowing and careful soil preparation; of seeding and planting special grains and legumes; of irrigating with water and husbanding with care the crops of forage that would feed the flocks" (Phillip Keller, A Shepherd Looks at Psalm 23, p. 45).

Jesus had done all that is necessary so we can "lie down" with Him. He promises rest to weary souls. "There remains therefore a rest for the people of God. For he who has entered His rest has himself also ceased from his works as God *did* from His. Let us therefore be diligent to enter that rest, lest anyone fall according to the same example of disobedience" (Hebrews 4:9-11).

When sheep lie down, there are conditions that have to be met. They must be:

• Free from fear.

Dogs, coyotes, cougars, bears are enemies of sheep. Phillip Keller related an incident of two dogs killing 292 sheep in one night. The psalmist makes it plain that He is there to protect us. "Yea, though I walk through the valley of the shadow of death, I will fear no evil; for You *are* with me; Your rod and Your staff, they comfort me" (Psalm 23:4).

- Free from torment by flies or parasites, and free from hunger.

Sheep lie down when free from fear, tension, hunger and aggravation. These fears are alleviated when the shepherd is near. We have the promise of inspiration that the Lord will never leave us. "Let your conduct *be* without covetousness; *be* content with such things as you have. For He Himself has said, 'I will never leave you nor forsake you'" (Hebrews 13:5).

"He Leads Me Beside Still Waters"

The source of water for sheep is dew on the grass, deep wells, or springs and streams. Sheep will not drink from a fast moving stream. A shepherd watering sheep by a stream will find a place to dam up the water so as to have a place where sheep can drink where the water is still.

As water nourishes the sheep physically, Christ nourishes us spiritually. Do you remember the story of Jesus speaking to the Samaritan woman at the well? "Jesus answered and said to her, "If you knew the gift of God, and who it is who says to you, 'Give Me a drink,' you would have asked Him, and He would have given you living water. The woman said to Him, 'Sir, You have nothing to draw with, and the well is deep. Where then do You get that living water? Are You greater than our father Jacob, who gave us the well, and drank from it himself, as well as his sons and his livestock?' Jesus answered and said to her, 'Whoever drinks of this water will thirst again, but whoever drinks of the water that I shall give him will never thirst. But the water that I shall give him will become in him a fountain of water springing up into everlasting life'" (John 4:10-14).

The analogy of this "spiritual water" is mentioned again in the Book of Revelation. John writes, "And he showed me a pure river of water of life, clear as crystal, proceeding from the throne of God and of the Lamb" (Revelation 22:1). "And He said to me, 'It is done! I am the Alpha and the Omega, the Beginning and the End. I will give of the fountain of the water of life freely to him who thirsts'" (Revelation 21:6). "And the Spirit and the bride say, 'Come!' And let him who hears say, 'Come!' And let him who thirsts come. Whoever desires, let him take the water of life freely" (Revelation 22:17).

"He Restores My Soul"

Sometimes sheep become "cast" and must be restored in order to survive. A "cast" sheep or a "cast down" sheep is one that cannot get up on his own. Keller says a cast sheep "is a very pathetic sight. Lying on its back, its feet in the air, it flays away frantically struggling to stand up, without success..." A heavy, fat, or long fleeced sheep will lie down comfortably in some little hollow or depression in the ground. It may roll on its side slightly to stretch out or relax. Suddenly, the center of gravity in the body shifts so that it turns on its back far enough that the feet no longer touch the ground. It may feel a sense of panic and start to paw frantically. Frequently, this only makes things worse. It rolls over even further. Now it is quite impossible for it to regain its feet" (Keller, ibid, pp. 60-61).

Keller lists three reasons for sheep to become cast. (1) The sheep looks for a soft, comfortable spot, rounded in the ground. (2) The sheep is literally weighed down with its own wool, often long and needing to be sheared. Sometimes it is matted with mud, manure or other things that weigh it down.

116

(3) The third cause of cast sheep is simply that they are too fat.

The sad thing about the analogy of our being sheep is that we can become cast Christians. When we look for a place to "take it easy" spiritually, we can become "cast Christians." Our God warned Israel about this: "Woe to you *who are* at ease in Zion, and trust in Mount Samaria, Notable persons in the chief nation, To whom the house of Israel comes" (Amos 6:1)!

Secondly, we also can become "cast Christians" when we are weighed down by our own problems—problems that keep us down and useless in the Lord's work.

Thirdly, we can become "cast Christians" when we are fattened with wealth and affluence, yet find ourselves spiritually bankrupt. Such was the case of the church at Laodicea. The Lord said, "Because you say, 'I am rich, have become wealthy, and have need of nothing'—and do not know that you are wretched, miserable, poor, blind, and naked" (Revelation 3:17). Often we find Christians who need a good shearing!

"He Leads Me In Paths Of Righteousness"

Sheep must be led. Without being led, sheep will stay in one place, feed in one area, and completely destroy the land. The land becomes impoverished and corrupted with disease and parasites. Again, quoting from Keller: "One need only travel through countries like Spain, Greece, Mesopotamia, North Africa and even parts of western United States and New Zealand or Australia to see the havoc wrought by sheep on the land (ibid, p. 70).

As Christians, we need a shepherd or we will wallow on the hills of sin and the valleys of decadence. The psalmist said it appropriately, "For He *is* our God, and we *are* the people of His pasture, and the sheep of His hand. Today, if you will hear His voice: 'Do not harden your hearts, as in the rebellion, as *in* the day of trial in the wilderness'" (Psalm 95:7-8). Also in Psalm 100:3, we are told, "Know that the LORD, He *is* God; *It is* He *who* has made us, and not we ourselves; w*e are* His people and the sheep of His pasture."

The tragedy of not allowing Jesus to be our Shepherd is seen when our Lord made the following observation: "But when He saw the multitudes, He was moved with compassion for them, because they were weary and scattered, like sheep having no shepherd" (Matthew 9:36). It is sad indeed, that today, so many are weary and scattered because they do not allow the Lord to be their Shepherd.

"Though I Walk Through The Valley Of Death"

We all have mountains and valleys in life. There are highs and lows. The lows (valleys) represent difficulties of life. It is interesting that when we pass through a particular valley, we can be consoled by those who have traveled the same valley—those who have been in similar situations. They are the ones best able to comfort. Whether death, discouragement, or a broken heart, when we walk through these valleys, it helps us to have someone with us who has been there before.

The same is true with death. Our Shepherd has been there before us. He knows the way and will lead us through the dark passes to eternal life. When we walk through the valley of death, we don't die there! We don't stop there! We walk through the valley of death!

There is a beautiful poem by Jane Eggleston titled "It's In the Valleys I Grow". Look it up on the internet and enjoy the beauty of the poem. Eggleston speaks of life's sorrows, troubles, woes, and pain and then turns to see Jesus on the cross. At this point, she asks God to forgive her for complaining because she knows what she is going through in life is nothing compared to the suffering of our Lord. She concludes with these words—"Thank you for valleys, Lord, for this one thing I know. The mountain tops are glorious, but it's in the valleys I grow!"

"Thy Rod And Staff Comfort Me"

The rod and staff of the shepherd are tools of the trade. The rod is a heavy stick, usually with a ball carved on one end, and used to throw at a predator or beat a predator off the sheep and therefore offer protection. The staff is a long stick with a crook on the end, used to move away thick brush and rescue a lost sheep. Both of these tools are sources of comfort to the sheep.

The rod and staff are figurative of power. The Christian can take comfort that our shepherd has protective power.

Our Shepherd, Jesus Christ, is not figurative of power but is the Power. God gave Him all authority. Authority is defined as "right, power, or jurisdiction." Before our Lord ascended back to heaven, He said, "All authority has been given to Me in heaven and on earth" (Matthew 28:18). Peter said that Jesus Christ is the "Shepherd and Overseer of your souls" (1 Peter 2:25).

"Thou Preparest A Table before Me In The Presence Of My Enemies"

In mountainous countries, there are high plateaus suitable for grazing sheep. They are called mesas. Mesa is the Spanish word for table. Shepherds must prepare these tables for the sheep to protect them. They must eradicate poisonous weeds that paralyze sheep and kill them. This preparing of the table is necessary for healthy sheep.

119

Also, the shepherd must clear out watering holes, springs and other sources of water supply. They must remove twigs, debris, rocks, etc., that have accumulated over the winter and blocked the water source. They may have to repair small dams in order to supply water.

Just as a shepherd will "prepare the table" for the sheep to eat and drink, our Lord, the Chief Shepherd (1 Peter 5:4), has prepared a table for us, represented in the Lord's Supper. We see that the Lord instituted this Supper in Matthew 26:26-28. The scripture says, "And as they were eating, Jesus took bread, blessed and broke *it,* and gave *it* to the disciples and said, "Take, eat; this is My body." Then He took the cup, and gave thanks, and gave *it* to them, saying, "Drink from it, all of you. For this is My blood of the new covenant, which is shed for many for the remission of sins."

For this reason, Christians gather to worship God and as a part of that worship, take the "Communion" or "The Lord's Supper."

"Thou Anointest My Head With Oil"

For centuries, shepherds have anointed the heads of their sheep with oil to ward off various species of flies and parasites that can literally torture sheep to death. The most disturbing is the nose fly that lays its eggs in the sheep's nose. The larvae hatch out and work their way up the nasal passages into the sheep's head, burrow into the flesh and cause intense irritation and inflammation. In biblical times, shepherds mixed olive oil, sulphur, and spices together and anointed the head and nose of the sheep.

Just as there are things that "bug" sheep, there are many things that "bug" us in life. But by focusing on our Shepherd, Jesus Christ, we can overcome and endure what life throws at us. We are told, "No temptation has overtaken you except such as is common to man; but God *is* faithful, who will not

120

allow you to be tempted beyond what you are able, but with the temptation will also make the way of escape, that you may be able to bear it. Therefore, my beloved, flee from idolatry" (1 Corinthians 10:13-14).

"My Cup Runs Over"

Shepherds would often draw water from a well and put it in cups for the sheep. The cups were stones with hollowed out places in the stones to hold water. These natural cups allowed the sheep to drink literally from a "cup." As the shepherd provides water to the point of overflowing or completely satisfying the thirst of the sheep, our Lord and Shepherd, Jesus Christ, is all we need. The metaphor is one of Christ meeting all of our spiritual needs fully and completely. He supplies what we need so that we "shall not want."

Why does the shepherd provide water for the sheep to the point of "overflowing" their cups? He does so because he cares. 1 Peter 5:7 says, "casting all your care on Him, for He cares for you."

"Surely Goodness and Mercy Shall Follow Me All the Days Of My Life"

This is the conclusion based on the preceding verses. The good shepherd provides those things that are good for the sheep and has mercy for them as they face the difficulties of their daily existence.

Our Shepherd (Jesus Christ) provides that which is good for us. Not only does He provide for us, He was willing to die for His sheep. "I am the Good Shepherd. The Good Shepherd gives His life for the sheep" (John 10:11). He did die for His sheep because of His great mercy for mankind, because of His great desire to save man and provide for him

121

a home in heaven. Psalm 106:1 says, "Praise the LORD! Oh, give thanks to the LORD, for He is good! For His mercy endures forever." This statement is repeated exactly in Psalms 107:1; 118:1; 118:29; 136:1. When the Lord tells us something once, we should believe it. When He tells us the same thing five times, we should really take it to heart.

"I Shall Dwell In The House Of The Lord Forever"

The above statement is a theme found in the Bible. The passages that show that the Lord wants to dwell with His people and that He wants His people to dwell with Him are too numerous to look at in this chapter.

One thing about this is certain; Jesus comforted His disciples by telling them that He would leave them, but would prepare a place for them so they could live with Him. He said, "Let not your heart be troubled; you believe in God, believe also in Me. In My Father's house are many mansions; if *it were* not *so,* I would have told you. I go to prepare a place for you. And if I go and prepare a place for you, I will come again and receive you to Myself; that where I am, *there* you may be also. And where I go you know, and the way you know" (John 14:1-4).

Conclusion

Each of us should be personally committed to having the Lord as "my" Shepherd. Indeed, He has done all that is necessary for my salvation. "There remains no more sacrifice for sins" (Hebrews 10:26).

We must indeed be very "Special to God" because we are "His people and the sheep of His pasture" (Psalm 100:3).

Chapter 11

You Are Special to God Because He Uses You to Influence Others for Good

"You are the light of the world. A city that is set on a hill cannot be hidden."

Matthew 5:14

Webster defines influence as "the power of persons or things to affect the character and actions of people." As God's people, we have the power to affect others in a very positive and good manner. If we do not use our influence the way God would have us to, we still have influence. However, this influence would be contrary to God and contrary to the influence we should have. We should remember that everyone has influence (good or bad). We must make sure we use our influence to help others see Christ living in us, and create in them a desire to be like Christ.

The Bible Teaches That We Have Influence

In the great Sermon on the Mount, Jesus talked about influence. He used two illustrations, salt and light, to make His point.

You are the salt of the earth. "You are the salt of the earth; but if the salt loses its flavor, how shall it be seasoned? It is then good for nothing but to be thrown out and trampled underfoot by men" (Matthew 5:13).

Salt has many purposes. Ninety-five percent of all salt is used, not to flavor food, but to preserve it. We, as Christians, are to preserve the earth, i.e., have an influence on it for good.

You are the light of the world. Not only does Jesus use the analogy of salt as a source of influence, He uses the analogy of light. "You are the light of the world. A city that is set on a hill cannot be hidden" (Matthew 5:14). Light shows the way through the darkness. Light influences darkness by dispelling it. Without light, we cannot see. Are you a "light of the world," living for Christ and doing His will?

Many years ago, someone made the point to me that there was a big difference in "letting your light shine" and "shining your light." His point was that many are shining their light, trying to let the world know how good they are, instead of "letting their light shine", that is, allowing the influence of Christ to be seen in what they do.

Noah, through his influence for good, preserved the world. In Genesis chapter six, we find that mankind had become evil in God's sight. The Lord "saw that the wickedness of man *was* great in the earth, and *that* every intent of the thoughts of his heart *was* only evil continually and the LORD was sorry that He had made man on the earth, and He was grieved in His heart" (Genesis 6:5-6). But the hope of mankind was found in verse 8. The Bible says, "But Noah found grace in the eyes of the Lord" (Genesis 6:8). It was through the influence of this good man that God determined to destroy the wicked world with a flood and start over with Noah and his family.

The right influence could have saved Sodom and Gomorrah. In Genesis, chapter 19, we have the story of the destruction of Sodom and Gomorrah. These cities could have been salvaged from their ungodliness if only ten righteous could have been found (Genesis 18:32). Because of a lack of influence for good, these cities were destroyed by God.

Moses influenced God to preserve His people. When the Children of Israel left the bondage of Egypt and proceeded to the Promised Land, they became discouraged and wanted to turn back to Egypt. When spies were sent to spy out the Land of Promise, they came back with a report that it was impossible to take the land. Because of their lack of faith, God determined that He would destroy the Israelites and make a nation of Moses. The Lord said, "I will strike them with the pestilence and disinherit them, and I will make of you a nation greater and mightier than they" (Numbers 14:12). At this point, Moses interceded for the Children of Israel and spoke to God on their behalf. Moses said, "Now *if* You kill these people as one man, then the nations which have heard of Your fame will speak, saying, 'Because the LORD was not able to bring this people to the land which He swore to give them, therefore He killed them in the wilderness.'" (Numbers 14:15-16). Moses continued by praying on their behalf, pleading to God's qualities of longsuffering, mercy and forgiveness. Because of the influence of Moses, God decided that He would not destroy the Israelites, but destroy all those who came out of Egypt (except Joshua and Caleb) in The Wilderness over a forty year period of wandering. The descendants of these people would be allowed to enter the Promised Land.

We can make a difference today! The moral condition of the world today is sufficient evidence of the need for the influence of God's people. The Proverbs writer said, "Righteousness exalts a nation, but sin is a reproach to any people" (Proverbs 14:34). But if we lose our influence, the Lord said, speaking of salt that loses its ability to influence, "It is then good for nothing but to be thrown out and trampled underfoot by men" (Matthew 5:13).

The Kingdom Of Heaven Is Like Leaven

"Another parable He spoke to them: 'The kingdom of heaven is like leaven, which a woman took and hid in three measures of meal till it was all leavened'" (Matthew 13:33). Leaven is a substance that influences or has an effect on another substance. For example, yeast will produce fermentation on dough or a liquid. We understand this when we see how yeast is used in flour and causes all the flour to lighten and rise. As yeast (or leavening) influences meal or flour, then we, as members of the Lord's Kingdom, the Lord's Church, should have influence on others for good. We are to overcome (influence) the world, not allow the world to overcome (influence) us. Jesus said, "For whatever is born of God overcomes the world. And this is the victory that has overcome the world— our faith" (1 John 5:4).

Leaven takes time to work. Many times we become discouraged when trying to influence others for good because we want instant success. Paul said, "And let us not grow weary while doing good, for in due season we shall reap if we do not lose heart" (Galatians 6:9).

Similar to the idea of overcoming the world, rather than allowing the world to overcome us, is the idea of conformity. We are told, "do not be conformed to this world, but be transformed by the renewing of your mind, that you may prove what is that good and acceptable and perfect will of God" (Romans 12:2).

In order to be transformed from the world, we are told "Do not love the world or the things in the world. If anyone loves the world, the love of the Father is not in him. For all that is in the world—the lust of the flesh, the lust of the eyes, and the pride of life—is not of the Father but is of the world. And the world is passing away, and the lust of it; but he who does the will of God abides forever" (1 John 2:15-17). We are also told by John, "Who is he who overcomes the world, but he who believes that Jesus is the Son of God" (1 John 5:5)?

On Whom Do We Have Influence?

We can influence those with whom we come into contact. People on the job or at school, neighbors, and those we conduct business with are people that we can influence for good. When we go to work, we need to remember that we are working for God, doing His will. The scriptures warn us about our influence at work, telling us that we are not to be guilty of eye service as men-pleasers, but "with good will doing service, as to the Lord, and not to men, knowing that whatever good anyone does, he will receive the same from the Lord, whether he is a slave or free" (Ephesians 6:7-8).

We influence others by our honesty and fairness. We are told that our conduct should be honorable among others that "they may, by your good works which they observe, glorify God in the day of visitation" (1 Peter 2:12).

How many times have you heard someone say, "I don't get mad, I get even!" But the Bible says that we are to "repay no one evil for evil. Have regard for good things in the sight of all men" (Romans 12:17). We are admonished "to lead a quiet life, to mind your own business, and to work with your own hands, as we commanded you, that you may walk properly toward those who are outside, and that you may lack nothing" (1Thessalonians 4:11-12). We are also told to provide "honorable things, not only in the sight of the Lord, but also in the sight of men" (2 Corinthians 8:21).

When it comes to having influence on our friends and our neighbors, we must remember the biblical admonition of being friendly. The Bible says, "A man who has friends must himself be friendly, but there is a friend who sticks closer than a brother" (Proverbs 18:24). The Bible also admonishes us to watch our speech. "Let no corrupt word proceed out of your mouth, but what is good for necessary edification, that it may impart grace to the hearers" (Ephesians 4:29). We are to use "sound speech that cannot be condemned, that one who is an opponent may be ashamed, having nothing evil to say of you" (Titus 2:8). The words we use are important and we will be held accountable for them in the Day of Judgment. Our Lord said, "But I say to you that for every idle word men may speak, they will give account of it in the Day of Judgment" (Matthew 12:36).

We can influence our children by raising them properly. Parents are to raise their children to be respectful. "And you, fathers, do not provoke your children to wrath, but bring them up in the training and admonition of the Lord" (Ephesians 6:4). We are to teach our children to obey us. "Children, obey your parents in all things, for this is well pleasing to the Lord. Fathers, do not provoke your children, lest they become discouraged" (Colossians 3:20-21). The

Bible says, "Train up a child in the way he should go, and when he is old he will not depart from it" (Proverbs 22:6).

As members of His church, we influence others by our regular worship. The writer of Hebrews tells us, "not forsaking the assembling of ourselves together, as is the manner of some, but exhorting one another, and so much the more as you see the Day approaching. For if we sin willfully after we have received the knowledge of the truth, there no longer remains a sacrifice for sins, but a certain fearful expectation of judgment, and fiery indignation which will devour the adversaries" (Hebrews 10:25-27).

As members of the church, we should help other Christians in time of need. When the churches in Judea were experiencing a severe famine, other churches contributed to the churches to help their members. Paul said, "Now concerning the collection for the saints, as I have given orders to the churches of Galatia, so you must do also: On the first day of the week let each one of you lay something aside, storing up as he may prosper, that there be no collections when I come" (1 Corinthians 16:1-2). Later, Paul commended the churches in Macedonia for their liberal contribution to the churches in Judea, even though the churches in Macedonia were experiencing poverty. Paul says, "Moreover, brethren, we make known to you the grace of God bestowed on the churches of Macedonia: that in a great trial of affliction the abundance of their joy and their deep poverty abounded in the riches of their liberality. For I bear witness that according to their ability, yes, and beyond their ability, they were freely willing, imploring us with much urgency that we would receive the gift and the fellowship of the ministering to the saints. And not only as we had hoped, but they first gave themselves to the Lord, and then to us by the will of God" (2 Corinthians 8:1-5).

Christians should also recognize their personal obligations in helping others. James says, "Pure and undefiled religion before God and the Father is this: to visit orphans and widows in their trouble, and to keep oneself unspotted from the world" (James 1:27).

We should grow spiritually in order to influence others spiritually. The apostle Paul, speaking of being spiritually minded as opposed to carnally minded, said, "For those who live according to the flesh set their minds on the things of the flesh, but those who live according to the Spirit, the things of the Spirit. For to be carnally minded is death, but to be spiritually minded is life and peace" (Romans 8:5-6).

We Influence Others After Our Death

The way we live our lives will have an influence, not only during our lives, but for many years after our deaths. John writes, "Then I heard a voice from heaven saying to me, 'Write:' 'Blessed are the dead who die in the Lord from now on.' 'Yes,' says the Spirit, 'that they may rest from their labors, and their works follow them'" (Revelation 14:13). The writer of the Book of Hebrews, in speaking of the righteousness of Abel, said that "he being dead still speaks" (Hebrews 11:4).

Our example will live on after we depart this life. Peter said, speaking of Christ, "For to this you were called, because Christ also suffered for us, leaving us an example, that you should follow His steps" (1 Peter 2:21).

Our influence, when our lives are over, will be either for good or evil. This is clearly seen in a study by Yale University on how the lifestyle of a person affects the lives of his or her children. The study focused on two men—Max Jukes and Jonathan Edwards. Jukes, an atheist, preached free sex, no laws, no formal education and no responsibilities. Edwards on the other hand was known as a disciplinarian. He was a Presbyterian minister with high moral standards, teaching that people should be responsible for their actions. Both of these men fathered thirteen children.

In a study of Max Jukes' descendants, it was found that there were 1,026 descendants. Among these descendants there were 300 convicts, 27 murderers, 190 prostitutes, and 509 alcoholics and drug addicts.

The descendants of Jonathan Edwards proved to be very different. Edwards had 929 descendants. Among these descendants were 430 ministers, 314 war veterans, 75 authors, 86 college professors, 13 university presidents, 7 congressmen, 3 governors, and a Vice-President of the United States. Certainly this study shows that, as the scripture says, "their works follow after them."

Conclusion

As children of God, we are to use our influence for good. Jesus said we are the "salt of the earth", the "light of the world" and the "leaven" in the kingdom. Let us do our part to influence as many as we can for good, that our good works might be a monument to a godly life.

God's people are special because of their relationship with God. God uses His people to influence others for good. When we use our influence for good, we are indeed, "Special to God!"

Chapter 12

You Are Special to God Because He Has Shown You the Unseen

"These all died in faith, not having received the promises, but having seen them afar off were assured of them, embraced them and confessed that they were strangers and pilgrims on the earth."

Hebrews 11:13

"Therefore we do not lose heart. Even though our outward man is perishing, yet the inward *man* is being renewed day by day. For our light affliction, which is but for a moment, is working for us a far more exceeding and eternal weight of glory, while we do not look at the things which are seen, but at the things which are not seen. For the things which are seen are temporary, but the things which are not seen are eternal" (2 Corinthians 4:16-18).

In this passage, we find Paul discussing something that seems unusual to us. Paul is talking about being able to see the unseen. Through the word of God, our Lord has allowed us to see some things in the future that many will not be able to see. It is only with the "eye of faith" that we can see these things, and those who do not have faith will not see them. We must be "Special to God" if He will allow us to see the unseen!

Why Some Cannot See The Unseen

Some look to the past. Some will never be able to see the unseen if they are always looking to the past. The things that happened in the past are clearly seen by all.

The scriptures warn us about looking back. Jesus said, "No one, having put his hand to the plow, and looking back, is fit for the kingdom of God" (Luke 9:62). The passage seems to illustrate for us the importance of knowing where you are going. How many times have you heard someone say to you, "Look where you are going?" Jesus is saying, "Go where you are looking!" If we are constantly looking back, we can't see where we are going. We can't see that which is in front of us. We can't see the future. We can't see the unseen.

The apostle Paul also warned about looking back. He said, "Brethren, I do not count myself to have apprehended; but one thing I do, forgetting those things which are behind and reaching forward to those things which are ahead, I press toward the goal for the prize of the upward call of God in Christ Jesus" (Philippians 3:13-14).

Some look to the present. If we are looking to the present, we are still seeing the things that are seen. Paul said, "while we do not look at the things which are seen, but at the things which are not seen, for the things which are seen *are* temporary, but the things which are not seen *are* eternal (2 Corinthains 4:18).

134

Some do not want to see the unseen. In 2 Peter 1, the apostle Peter tells us that some people are nearsighted (spiritually), even to (spiritual) blindness. The reason for this is that they have forgotten some things, some important things about spiritual development after one becomes a Christian. Notice what Peter says, "But also for this very reason, giving all diligence, add to your faith virtue, to virtue knowledge, to knowledge self-control, to self-control perseverance, to perseverance godliness, to godliness brotherly kindness, and to brotherly kindness love. For if these things are yours and abound, *you will be* neither barren nor unfruitful in the knowledge of our Lord Jesus Christ. For he who lacks these things is shortsighted, even to blindness, and has forgotten that he was cleansed from his old sins. Therefore, brethren, be even more diligent to make your call and election sure, for if you do these things you will never stumble; for so an entrance will be supplied to you abundantly into the everlasting kingdom of our Lord and Savior Jesus Christ" (2 Peter 1:5-11).

How Can We See The Unseen?

The Bible teaches that we can see the unseen through the eye of faith. "Now faith is the substance of things hoped for, the evidence of things not seen. For by it the elders obtained a *good* testimony. By faith we understand that the worlds were framed by the word of God, so that the things which are seen were not made of things which are visible" (Hebrews 11:1-3). The apostle Paul said, "For we were saved in this hope, but hope that is seen is not hope; for why does one still hope for what he sees? But if we hope for what we do not see, we eagerly wait for *it* with perseverance" (Romans 8:24-25).

Let us now look at some biblical examples of men who were able to see the unseen.

135

Noah saw the unseen. Noah had never seen a flood and there is good evidence that he had never seen rain, but through the eye of faith, God allowed Noah to see the coming destruction of the earth. "By faith Noah, being divinely warned of things not yet seen, moved with godly fear, prepared an ark for the saving of his household, by which he condemned the world and became heir of the righteousness which is according to faith" (Hebrews 11:7). Because Noah believed what God said about the impending destruction of the world, Noah was motivated to build a gigantic ark, saving his family and the animals of the earth.

Abraham saw the unseen. Abraham's faith in God allowed him to not only seek a land that God promised him, but also allowed Abraham to see a heavenly land that was promised to him. "By faith Abraham obeyed when he was called to go out to the place which he would receive as an inheritance. And he went out, not knowing where he was going. By faith he dwelt in the land of promise as *in* a foreign country, dwelling in tents with Isaac and Jacob, the heirs with him of the same promise; for he waited for the city which has foundations, whose builder and maker *is* God" (Hebrews 11:8-10). In verse thirteen, we read, "These all died in faith, not having received the promises, but having seen them afar off were assured of them, embraced *them* and confessed that they were strangers and pilgrims on the earth."

Moses saw the unseen. Another biblical character who was able to see the unseen was Moses. He could see where the riches of Egypt would lead him and where service to God would lead him. The Bible says, "By faith Moses, when he became of age, refused to be called the son of Pharaoh's daughter, choosing rather to suffer affliction with the people of God than to enjoy the passing pleasures of sin, esteeming the reproach of Christ greater riches than the treasures in

Egypt; for he looked to the reward. By faith he forsook Egypt, not fearing the wrath of the king; for he endured as seeing Him who is invisible" (Hebrews 11:24-27).

For What Should We Look?

We should look for the hope in Christ. Paul told Titus that he should be "looking for the blessed hope and glorious appearing of our great God and Savior Jesus Christ, who gave Himself for us, that He might redeem us from every lawless deed and purify for Himself *His* own special people, zealous for good works" (Titus 2:13-14).

We should be looking for heaven. Peter tells us that at the end of time the earth and all things therein will be burned up. In light of this, he says, "looking for and hastening the coming of the day of God, because of which the heavens will be dissolved, being on fire, and the elements will melt with fervent heat" (2 Peter 3:12). The Bible tells us that there is a time coming when Christians shall be comforted. "And God will wipe away every tear from their eyes; there shall be no more death, nor sorrow, nor crying. There shall be no more pain, for the former things have passed away" (Revelation 21:4).

Things We Can See That We Don't Want To See

The Bible teaches in Romans 10:17 that "faith comes by hearing and hearing by the word of God." As we study the word of God, we learn that our future may not be as bright and blissful as we, perhaps, would like it to be. As we understand our eventual future, we see the need to conform to God's will in order to be pleasing to Him. If we fail to do so, our future will be bleak indeed.

We don't want to see the wrath of God. While the Bible tells us "God is love" (1 John 4:8), many religious leaders fail to mention that God is a God of wrath and vengence. His wrath and vengence will be experienced by those who fail to do His will. Paul said in the Book of Romans, "For the wrath of God is revealed from heaven against all ungodliness and unrighteousness of men, who suppress the truth in unrighteousness, because what may be known of God is manifest in them, for God has shown *it* to them. For since the creation of the world His invisible attributes are clearly seen, being understood by the things that are made, *even* His eternal power and Godhead, so that they are without excuse" (Romans 1:18-20). Later in the scriptures, we read, "Let no one deceive you with empty words, for because of these things the wrath of God comes upon the sons of disobedience" (Ephesians 5:6).

The God of vengeance is mentioned in 2 Thessalonians 1:7-9, where Paul says, "and to give you who are troubled rest with us when the Lord Jesus is revealed from heaven with His mighty angels, in flaming fire taking vengeance on those who do not know God, and on those who do not obey the gospel of our Lord Jesus Christ. These shall be punished with everlasting destruction from the presence of the Lord and from the glory of His power."

Yes, this God of love is also a God of wrath and vengeance. This attribute of God should compel us to serve Him. "Vengeance is Mine, I will repay, says the Lord" (Romans 12:19).

If unprepared for judgment, we will not want to experience the Judgment of God. One of the clear and repeated teachings of the Bible is that there will be a judgment in which God will separate the saved from the lost. As stated earlier in this book, The Judgment is as real as anything you will experience in this life. Judgment is mentioned 312 times in the Bible and is therefore an important biblical topic. The "Day of Judgment" is mentioned eleven times in the New Testament.

The final judgment of God is not a subject that people want to think about, but the Bible says we will all be there and give an account of the lives we have lived. Speaking of this judgment, Jesus said, "When the Son of Man comes in His glory, and all the holy angels with Him, then He will sit on the throne of His glory. All the nations will be gathered before Him, and He will separate them one from another, as a shepherd divides *his* sheep from the goats. And He will set the sheep on His right hand, but the goats on the left" (Matthew 25:31-33).

Our Lord goes on to say to those on the right hand, "Come, you blessed of My Father, inherit the kingdom prepared for you from the foundation of the world" (Matthew 25:34).

But to those on the left hand, the Lord will say, "Depart from Me, you cursed, into the everlasting fire prepared for the devil and his angels" (Matthew 25:41).

Who then will be saved? Jesus answers this question for us. "Not everyone who says to Me, 'Lord, Lord,' shall enter the kingdom of heaven, but he who does the will of My Father in heaven" (Matthew 7:21).

In light of this judgment that we will all experience, we need to adhere to the admonition of our Lord, "Watch therefore: for you do not know what hour your Lord is coming" (Matthew 24:42).

Conclusion

Can you see the unseen today? Can you see heaven and its glories? Can you see Christ on the right hand of God? Can you picture the throne scene in heaven? Do you look to heaven each day? If you haven't been able to do this, you need to practice seeing the unseen. Do you look for spiritual things? Consider again the words of Paul. "While we do not look at the things which are seen, but at the things which are not seen. For the things which are seen *are* temporary, but the things which are not seen *are* eternal" (2 Corinthians 4:18).

Surely, we must be "Special to God" if He allows us to see the unseen!

Epilogue

We live in a world that is truly "looking for love in all the wrong places." We need to be loved. Sometimes friends and family, co-workers and fellow Christians fail in helping us to have this special feeling. But you can be assured that you are loved. God loves you. He loves you so much that He allowed His only Son to die for you so you might live with Him throughout all eternity.

As you travel life's journey and search for meaning in your life, remember the words of the Preacher. "Let us hear the conclusion of the whole matter: Fear God and keep His commandments, for this is man's all" (Ecclesiastes 12:13).

Do you know someone who needs to feel the love of the Lord? Then share this book with them. Remind them that they are "special!"

I hope you have enjoyed this book and perhaps you can now look at your life differently, being assured that you are indeed, "Special to God." As previously stated, we are "special", not because of who we are, but of who God is and because God's people have a special relationship with Him.

LaVergne, TN USA
14 October 2010
200756LV00003B/4/P